D0941915

MacARTHUR: The Life of a General

MacARTHUR: The Life of a General

by ALLEN PHELPS JULIAN

for the Editors, the *Army Times*

DUELL, SLOAN AND PEARCE

New York

First edition

Affiliate of
MEREDITH PRESS
Des Moines & New York

Library of Congress Catalogue Card Number 63-20603

Manufactured in the United States of America for Meredith Press

VAN REES PRESS • NEW YORK

To the American front-line combat soldier,
who knew Douglas MacArthur best

✗ The author wishes to acknowledge the generous help of the following gentlemen in his preparation of the material for *MacArthur: The Life of a General:* H. R. Baukhage of the Army Times Publishing Company; Major General Courtney Whitney, USA (Ret.); Colonel Lewis S. Sorley, USA (Ret.), USMA 1891; Captain Bernard W. Abrams, USA (Ret.), USMA 1947; Togo Watanabe, Princeton, 1913; Tom Clifft Campbell, USMA 1946; and Dr. L. Minor Blackford.

The author is especially indebted to A. A. Hoehling, Book Editor of the Army Times Publishing Company, without whose experienced and patient guidance he would have gone far astray.

He also wishes to thank the following libraries for their kind assistance: Atlanta Historical Society, Atlanta Public Library, Army-Navy Club Library, Library of Congress, National Archives, and U.S. Army Library.

CONTENTS

ILLUSTRATIONS

following page 116

MacARTHUR: The Life of a General

1.

THE BOY COLONEL OF THE WEST

✗ *"In the Army there's sobriety, promotion's very slow!"*
On the morning of January 27, 1880, at Little Rock Barracks, Arkansas, Captain Arthur MacArthur, 13th Infantry, had been a Captain more than thirteen years. He could listen with wry appreciation to this old favorite song of the West Pointers in the regiment and wonder why he had forsaken a promising future in civilian life.

Yet seldom had there been a more dedicated soldier than Arthur MacArthur. It never occurred to him that the son who had been born the night before—and who would be christened "Douglas"—might follow any other career.

"I started Douglas toward West Point the day he was born," he told his aide, Captain Peyton C. March, many

3

years later. He was confident that his sons would follow the flag.

He was not disappointed. But, on that bleak January day, when the officers of the garrison were smoking his cigars, and their ladies were cooing over his day-old son, he could hardly have foreseen the heights to which this son would rise; that he would someday become one of the most controversial of great American soldiers; that he would conquer and rule a mighty Asiatic nation whose people would come to look upon him as their own; or that he would finally sacrifice himself in a vain effort to save his country from its first military defeat.

Although not a graduate himself, Arthur MacArthur was deeply imbued with the spirit of the West Point Code—Duty, Honor, Country. He had sought an appointment. He was not quite seventeen when, in May of 1862, he gained an interview with President Lincoln. But all of the Presidential appointments for the year had been made. "Next year," Mr. Lincoln promised him.

Back home, impatience gripped him. The Civil War was in its second year. Boys no older than himself were serving in Virginia and Tennessee. He was determined to join them.

Reluctantly Judge Arthur MacArthur gave his consent. A new regiment, the 24th Wisconsin Volunteer Infantry, was being formed. So when, in August, it was mustered into Federal service, his son was on its rolls as a First Lieutenant and adjutant of the regiment. He was two months past seventeen.

At Perryville and at Stone's River, Arthur was cited "for gallantry under fire." At Missionary Ridge he won the Medal of Honor, the country's highest award for valor, "for coolness and conspicuous bravery in seizing the colors of his regiment and planting them on the enemy's works."

In January, 1864, he was promoted to Major over the heads of several Captains. On May 14, after the severe fighting at Resaca, in General Sherman's Georgia campaign, he was the senior officer left in the regiment. As such he assumed command. He was not quite nineteen, but there was no thought of appointing an older commander.

The Battle of Franklin, Tennessee, won him a brevet promotion to Colonel, but it was his last battle. Severe wounds kept him from the fighting until the war was almost over.

In June, 1865, the "Boy Colonel of the West," as he had become widely known, led his battle-shrunken regiment home to be mustered out of service. At twenty he was a veteran regimental commander whose career had already ended.

He began to study law, but the Colors and the Code had captured him ... these and the habit of command. Finally their call became too strong. By July of 1866 he was a Captain in the regular Army.

Eight years of hard service followed, all on the western frontier. It was a harsh and dangerous life, but he set about acquiring the education of which the war had deprived him. Even in the rough and noisy atmosphere of bachelor quarters, his studies were never neglected.

Despite his youth, he was sympathetic with the plight of the plains Indians, who had become tragic victims of white avarice and deceit. Later this trait enabled him to deal wisely with the people of the Philippines, a fighting race whose affection and trust he won completely.

Late in 1874 MacArthur's Company K was sent to Jackson Barracks, near New Orleans. Although the blue uniform was hardly an entree to New Orleans society so soon after the Civil War, he made friends. Not that society claimed all of his off-duty time; the habits of study had become too firmly fixed.

New Orleans' famed Mardi Gras festival had hardly begun when he met the first girl to whom he had ever given more than casual attention. Lovely, Virginia-born Mary Pinkney Hardy had come down from Norfolk to spend the season with friends. She was twenty-two. Sweet, soft-voiced, deceptively shy, she captivated the young bachelor Captain, whose blue uniform bespoke a war record alien to her heritage.

"Pinky," as her family called her, was staunchly Confederate. Her brothers had served under Lee. Outwardly she was cool to Arthur; but, behind her mask of indifference, she was captivated, too. For the first time Arthur's studies were neglected. Life had suddenly gained a completely new dimension. He was in love.

Even from his slender pay his savings had been substantial. His family was proud of its lineage. As chiefs of the Clan Campbell, the MacArthurs had a colorful place in ancient Scottish lore. He had lived cleanly. In any other profession he would have felt free to speak. He hesitated to ask her to share the hardships and the uncertainties of a life which could offer her little but possible early widowhood.

How he found the courage is not a matter of record; but it has long been believed that, in this campaign, he had the subtle support of the enemy. Later he learned that, despite her shyness, Mary possessed an unusual fund of firm determination. And he learned that she had a way of accomplishing what she set out to do. Her youngest son inherited these characteristics.

In a few weeks Arthur was granted leave and went up to Riveredge, the old Hardy home near Norfolk. Mary's father, Dr. Thomas Hardy, and her mother received him cordially. Her brothers were less friendly. With them the wounds of war had not yet healed.

On May 19, 1875, they were married. Mary's brothers did not attend the wedding. Although she was disappointed, she was still enough of a Confederate to understand.

On August 1, 1876, their first son was born. Following age-old MacArthur tradition, he was named Arthur. On October 17, 1878, a second son, Malcolm, was born. Douglas was born on January 26, 1880. There were no more children.

It was a proud morning; but Arthur MacArthur would have been doubly proud could he have known how deeply the seeds of his cherished Code had been sown in his infant son. Douglas would follow the flag. He, too, would serve his country faithfully and well. The shining tenets of Duty, Honor, and Country would guide him throughout his years. To the Clan Campbell, a new MacArthur chieftain had been born.

2.

THE SOUND OF A BUGLE

☓ In her first five years as an army wife Mary MacArthur had made five moves and borne three sons. Autumn of 1880 found them at Fort Wingate, 150 miles west of Albuquerque, on the Continental Divide.

They were deep in Indian country. Any dawn might find a strong war party storming the rough stockade and flaming arrows firing sun-dried roofs. Yet there was gaiety and laughter, and colorful sunsets lent a spectacular note to the day's ending.

Late in 1882 they took a long leave. After weeks of travel they reached Norfolk and Riveredge. Mary's brothers had become reconciled to their Yankee brother-in-law, and welcomed him warmly.

Early in April the boys were stricken with virulent measles. Little Malcolm died. When Arthur and Douglas were able to travel, the saddened family began their long journey back to Fort Wingate.

Another move awaited them. Company K was ordered to Fort Selden, a bleak, one-company post on the Rio Grande, thirty miles above El Paso. It was a cold three-hundred-mile march but, snug in a covered wagon, Mary and the boys traveled in relative comfort. Always alert for roving war parties, Arthur marched with his men.

It was a lonely station. The only other women were the company laundresses—wives of soldiers in Company K—and occasional curious squaws. The quarters were flat-roofed, one-story adobes, whose backs formed part of the stockade. Yet Mary managed to make them cheerful.

Her time was fully occupied. There were two quick young minds to be guided constructively . . . two eager curiosities to be satisfied. Both Mary and Arthur devoted themselves to these tasks, and to the boys' spiritual development as well.

Unquestionably the two most powerful influences in the shaping of Douglas MacArthur were his father and his mother. Each possessed great strength of character. In their complete harmony, they created an atmosphere of love and security. Their wise teachings, and their strict insistence upon daily study achievements, laid the foundation for the impressive intellect which would later enable him to grasp intricate problems with seeming ease and to reach flawless decisions.

They began early to implant in each young mind a firm sense of obligation . . . of justice, loyalty, and right. As they developed, the precepts of Duty, Honor, and Country became instinctive.

The boys absorbed other never-to-be-forgotten lore.

"My earliest childhood recollection," Douglas MacArthur said in later years, "is the sound of a bugle." He retained other impressions. For a small boy, life on a frontier army post was one of endless excitement. It was peopled with colorful figures—soldiers, Indians, cowboys, scouts. He remembered the tales of the soldiers . . . of Indian campaigns under Gibbon or Crook, and of Civil War battles under Grant or Sherman . . . or "Old Joe" Johnston or Lee.

Douglas had been born into the Army. Now a lasting love of the Army was being born in him. His mother encouraged this bending of the twig. She told him stories which swelled his pride in his father. She encouraged him to work hard so that he, too, could become a great soldier . . . "as distinguished as General Lee." In his eyes his father was a dashing and romantic figure, and the bravest soldier of them all. Someday he would be like him.

From his father Douglas inherited splendid traits—courage, logic, a liberal viewpoint, rigid self-discipline. From his mother he inherited more. It was already apparent that he would resemble her. He, too, would be tall and slender, with dark hair and expressive hands. He, too, would be complex. In him her vivid imagination was born afresh. Like her, he could be calm and alertly practical deep inside himself, no matter what surface emotions might be stirred. It would be her instincts, her talents, that would fix his eyes on the stars.

3.

TO WEST POINT

✗ In the fall Company K moved to Fort Leavenworth, Kansas.

In their new home, the boys found a strange and exciting world. Ten-year-old Arthur fitted easily into the sixth grade. Douglas, who would be seven in January, was accepted readily in the second. They had been well prepared.

It was a new experience to have playmates. They learned games and made friends . . . after they had won acceptance. To Arthur's delight, each took attempted bullying in stride. As one neighbor put it, they were "manly little boys." Each could stand his ground.

Early in 1889 Arthur's fortunes changed. A vacancy occurred in a staff corps which he was strongly recommended to fill. On July 1 he was appointed a Major in the Adjutant General's Department. In a few more days he would have been a captain for twenty-three years.

Well before time for the schools to open, the MacArthurs were settled in Washington. At first the boys were awed by their new surroundings. They missed the color and excitement of garrison life. But when school opened they again fitted easily into appropriate grades and made new friends.

In June of 1892 Arthur, Junior, entered the Naval Academy. His heart was in the Navy. His father had hoped that he would enter West Point, but when he learned Arthur's real preference he was mollified.

In October, 1893, Major MacArthur was assigned to duty at San Antonio, Texas, and again a new world opened for Douglas. He entered the West Texas Military Academy as a day student. He lacked three months of being fourteen. It was not easy to fit into a class which had completed seven weeks of study, but he did—and thrived on the challenge. His parents' training had readied him for competitive efforts.

Some of the older cadets made life miserable for the late-coming freshman, but he took it in good grace. He soon proved that he could hold his own, and before the year was over he had shown his ability to excel in athletics as well as in scholarship.

Although slender, he was physically tough. He developed into a fast shortstop on the baseball team, which he later managed. Despite his lack of weight, he played good football. Nerve, quick thinking, and a compelling will made him a dependable quarterback. During his four years at West Texas these teams lost only one game each. His teammates gave him generous credit for these successes.

Scholastically he lived up to his father's expectations. His four yearly averages were 96.3, 95.15, 97.65, and 97.33. Not only did he stand at the top of the Class of 1897, he won the school's highest award—the Academy Gold Medal. He also won the Lockwood Silver Medal for excellence in elocution . . . his first flight into oratory.

In May, 1896, Arthur MacArthur had been promoted to Lieutenant Colonel, just thirty-one years after his first promotion to that grade. Late in 1897 he was transferred to St. Paul. His legal residence was in Milwaukee, the family home. To assure Douglas' eligibility for an appointment to West Point from Wisconsin, his wife and son established residence there. Colonel MacArthur went on to St. Paul alone, the beginning of a long separation.

One worry haunted him—despite his athletic prowess, Douglas had a slight curvature of the spine. Unless it could be corrected, it would bar him from admission to West Point.

In April, 1898, war was declared against Spain. Arthur MacArthur was appointed a Brigadier General of volunteers and sent to the Philippine Islands.

As the months passed Douglas' curvature was corrected. Months of intensive study, under his mother's devoted guidance, prepared him for the stiff competitive examinations.

He had grown tall. On June 3 the report of his physical examination showed him to be 5 feet, 10¼ inches tall and to weigh 133 pounds. He had thick, dark hair and brown eyes, which were soft when his face was in repose, but which could be unusually penetrating for one so young, a characteristic enhanced by a sharp, aquiline nose.

In the mental examinations he led the field. His average was 93.3; that of his nearest competitor, 77.9.

HE WILL GO TO WEST POINT, the Milwaukee *Journal* reported on the 7th. ". . . He accomplished his mission with a big margin to spare."

He was nineteen years and four months old. At that age his father had been in command of his regiment for nearly five months.

Out in the Philippines, General MacArthur was gaining new fame. Under his experienced command, his brigade had opened the way to Manila, which fell on August 13. Immediately he was promoted to Major General to rank from that date.

For years the Filipinos had been fighting for independence. They were rid of one set of masters and did not want another. They were tough, intelligent, and determined to be free. In February, 1899, they attacked Manila with a force far outnumbering the American garrison. They were defeated, but a costly war had begun—the Philippine Insurrection.

His success in defeating the Insurrectos, and in restoring peace, made General MacArthur's name familiar in every American household. It was under the shadow of his father's spreading fame that Douglas entered West Point.

4.

HEAD OF THE CLASS OF 1903

✘ Douglas MacArthur's arrival at West Point foreshadowed things to come. Immediately he became the object of critical attention. He tried to be self-effacing, but his father's successes against the Insurrectos—which the papers played up daily—made him a marked man.

He received special attention from the beast detail, whose task it was to reduce the newly arrived plebes to one common social denominator. He was reminded repeatedly that, while his father might be a great soldier, he was less than nothing.

Southern upperclassmen took special delight in making him recite his father's battlefield exploits against the "rebels."

Despite himself, his carriage and self-assurance gave him an air of arrogance. He was subjected to continual petty hazing, which he took in good grace. But he had self-control, and he was determined to show no personal feelings which might be mistaken for weakness.

In summer camp the plebes were hazed by the yearlings, who had just completed their own plebe year and were eager to inflict upon the new plebes the indignities which they had suffered.

Several yearlings were determined to break Douglas down. He was "exercised" until he almost fainted from physical exhaustion.

When it was over, he was shaken with convulsions, but he refused to permit his alarmed tentmate to request medical aid. With a blanket stuffed in his mouth to check involuntary moans, he suffered it out. In the morning he was almost too weak to stand. Will power enabled him to get through the day without revealing his condition.

Word of the affair spread quickly through the cadet body. Aware that they had gone too far, the guilty yearlings wondered tensely what the mistreated plebe would do. He remained silent.

In June, 1900, the beginning of his yearling year, Douglas was made a cadet corporal. When the scholastic standings for the year were posted, he stood first in his class.

Meanwhile, his father had been appointed Military Governor of the Philippines. He had not yet brought the insurrection to a close; but its leader, Emilio Aguinaldo, had been captured and, to his amazement, treated with courtesy. General MacArthur invited Aguinaldo's family to join him, and shocked Caucasian society by treating them as social equals.

Won over by MacArthur's liberal attitude, Aguinaldo advised his followers to give up the useless struggle. Diehard

Insurrectos would continue to waylay small parties of Americans, but the insurrection was almost ended.

In Douglas, personal traits began now to manifest themselves. He was a stickler for perfection. It took a sharp-eyed "tac" to find anything wrong with the appearance of members of his squad.

He met issues head on, but he was always fair. And no one ever complained of having been treated unjustly. He had long since determined that he would never condone hazing. He studied intensely. Yet he found time for other things. He played baseball for two years. In two games against the navy team, he scored a run in each.

He did not go out for the football team. Baseball was his better game, and he could not spare the time for both and still attain the military and academic goals which he had set for himself. But, in his final year, he managed the football team.

He had complete confidence in his ability to master any subject and to meet any situation; yet he had not overcome his shyness. He preferred the companionship of one or two chosen friends to that of a group. Although he enjoyed the cadet "hops" and the company of girls, he was no ladies' man. As he grew older the gayest of social functions bored and repelled him.

Like most shy persons, his mannerisms were sometimes exaggerated, and he had already begun to employ the rather dramatic phrasing which, in later years, would raise critical eyebrows.

At the end of his yearling year he had again headed his class, and he was made first sergeant of Company A. At the end of his second class, or junior year, he had dropped to third place. But when the list of new appointments was announced, he was named as "First Captain," the cadet's highest military honor.

Years later, a plebe would recall him as "a tall, slender, handsome cadet, immaculate with maroon silk sash, plumed dress hat, glinting sword, and four gold stripes of chevrons. His movements were almost dashing . . . and his commands were sharp and ringing. He displayed an odd quickness of gesture, buoyancy of gait, and cheeriness of expression."

During his First Captaincy the discipline of the Corps of Cadets "was never tighter." But despite his zeal as a disciplinarian, he had already acquired the successful officer's knack of sometimes looking the other way.

On one "hop" night several upperclassmen were conspicuously absent from the floor. Cadet Captain MacArthur found them in a vacant room shooting craps. The guilty cadets sprang to attention, but he appeared to see nothing unusual.

"If you gentlemen don't stop boning so hard," he advised them straight-facedly, "you will be seeing spots before your eyes."

In religious matters he was devout but not a formalist. He was never sacrilegious. Like General Sherman, he believed firmly in the "main doctrines of the Christian religion [and] the purity of its morals," but after graduation he seldom attended religious services. All through life, however, he rendered fervent thanks to his Creator for having brought him through turmoil and danger, safely and with success to the American arms.

Like his mother, he was highly intuitive. He could see into the heart of a problem and form a quick conclusion.

In June, 1903, Douglas MacArthur graduated at the head

of his class. He was First Captain, first in scholastic standing, and first in the affections of the Corps of Cadets. He was the class valedictorian and the cadet voted the most likely to succeed. He was the head of the student body.

His final average for the four years, in sixteen subjects, was 98.14, the highest, all things considered, in West Point's first 101 years. His records in English, history, and law were perfect. He excelled in mathematics, the sciences, and in both civil and military engineering. His lowest average was in drawing—90.4.

School days behind them, the Class of 1903 shook hands all around and "said farewell to cadet gray to don the army blue." It was not destined to become a widely known class, but it served the nation faithfully and well.

"Of all of the groups with which I have been associated," Douglas MacArthur said later, "this is the one I most cherish."

5.

SURVEYING BATAAN

✗ His class standing qualified Second Lieutenant MacArthur to choose the Corps of Engineers. Promotion was less slow in the "Corps Divine," as less favored wags had dubbed it, and its duties were more stimulating to an active mind.

In September he was en route to Manila. His year in the islands took him to Samar, Panay, Cebu, and Leyte on road building, surveying, and wharf and sea-wall construction. Back on Luzon, he led a surveying party which mapped portions of a locality that he would later make famous—the Bataan Peninsula.

As he came to know them, he developed a faith in the Philippine people which was never shaken. Among them he made friendships which stood the test of war. Gradually he began to share his father's vision of a proudly independent Philippine nation . . . of a people who, in a very few decades, would rise from the semibarbarism in which the Spanish had enslaved them.

Through the years old soldiers have told the tale of Mac-Arthur's first exposure to enemy fire.

On a remote jungle trail his surveying party was ambushed. A sergeant walking beside him was struck by a charge of buckshot. Instinctively MacArthur caught the sergeant as he fell. As MacArthur bent over, a second charge tore off his campaign hat. Had he remained erect, it would have blown off the top of his head.

Later, when the guerrillas had been routed and a badly shaken MacArthur had his party moving forward again, another sergeant now walking beside him said, "Begging the Lieutenant's pardon, but I would like to assure the Lieutenant that, from here on in, his life is all on velvet!"

From that day to Korea, innumerable—sometimes reckless —exposures to enemy fire have borne out the sergeant's prophesy.

On April 23, 1904, he was promoted to First Lieutenant. Later that year he was ordered home for duty in San Francisco. He left the islands reluctantly. He had succumbed to their lure.

Three months after his arrival his father passed through San Francisco en route to Tokyo for duty as the chief American observer with the Japanese Army in Manchuria. In October, 1905, General MacArthur received a far broader assignment. His reports of affairs in Japan and Manchuria had stirred the interest of President Theodore Roosevelt. They were not limited to military matters, but included analyses of the resources of each country and its probable long-range goals. Now he was to make a military and economic survey of conditions throughout the Far East. His son was ordered to accompany him as his aide.

Nine months of travel took them from Tokyo to Bombay, and from the Khyber Pass to Java. He saw at first hand the weaknesses of the Oriental countries ... and their latent strengths.

He learned to appreciate the Oriental mind. Later he trained himself to think in ways which would impress that mind. He gained impressions which influenced him in later years. He learned, for example, that, to the people of the Orient, the Russians are an Oriental people.

He came to share his father's conviction that, as the years passed, the greatest threat to America's security would come from Asia rather than from any combination of European powers.

Various assignments followed—the Engineer School at Fort Belvoir, a few months in the White House as the junior military aide to the President, routine duty in Washington and at Fort Leavenworth. At Leavenworth he met another highly promising young officer—Captain George Catlett Marshall. Neither was attracted to the other.

Douglas spent four years at Leavenworth. Although he was not assigned as a student, he attended lectures and sat in on discussions. Study took up most of his evenings, although he attended an occasional party. At infrequent stag affairs he would resonantly sing his favorite song: "Old Soldiers Never Die." Occasionally he sat in on a mild game of poker. Sometimes he took a drink.

He played on the officers' baseball team, which he also

managed. On one occasion he slyly entertained the visiting Kansas City Country Club team so lavishly at luncheon that, dulled by food and drink, they were easily beaten. Next year they outfoxed him by letting him entertain the wrong players. The third year, to everyone's amusement, he won the play-off by introducing two presentable young semipro players as recent West Point graduates.

On February 27, 1911, he was promoted to Captain. For a while he was assigned to duty as an instructor. A fellow instructor complained of the annoyance of the question-and-answer period following each lecture. Douglas explained how he had avoided the nuisance.

"At the end of my first lecture, I tell the group that I am ready to answer questions. But before I yield the floor, I tell them that, in my father's opinion, question askers fall into three groups. The first are too lazy to dig up the answers themselves. The second are the spotlight seekers, who want favorable attention. The third are the ones who want to haze the instructor. Then I ask, 'Are there any questions?' "

On the morning of September 6, 1912, a wire brought news of his father's death: he had been stricken while addressing a reunion of the old 24th Wisconsin. He had died "at the head of his regiment."

His father's passing created a new problem—a home for his mother. He wanted to be with her again, but she was in bad health. The climate at Fort Leavenworth was not likely to improve it. Duty in Washington would make the Army's finest medical talent available to her.

It took some doing, and he angered several seniors, but in November he was ordered to Washington for duty. A few days later he and his mother were comfortably settled there.

Major General Leonard Wood, the Chief of Staff, was looking for promising young general staff officer material. Shrewd, aggressive, practical, Wood valued these qualities in others. Captain MacArthur soon caught his eye.

General Wood was soon satisfied that he had found a young officer who was well grounded in military doctrine and who could think independently. It was his custom to require various officers to study matters that required his decision and to suggest appropriate actions. He found that Captain MacArthur frequently disagreed with his seniors, and that he was not afraid to express contrary opinions. In many cases he accepted MacArthur's recommendations.

It was a matter of great satisfaction to MacArthur, but it exacted a price. In winning the approval of the Chief of Staff, he had won also the cordial dislike of many important seniors. It would not be the last time in a long and unusual career.

In April, 1914, United States troops, under the command of Major General Frederick Funston, were sent to seize and occupy the city of Vera Cruz, Mexico. On the 22nd it was decided that Captain MacArthur should be sent there as an observer. He would report to General Wood and the War Department.

Upon arrival in Vera Cruz he called on General Funston. In the meantime confidential orders had reached Funston which limited his zone of occupation to the immediate environs of the city, and his activities to purely defensive measures. Under no circumstances was any action to be taken which might increase tension.

Since General Funston had seen no reason to inform Mac-

Arthur of this directive, the latter felt free to use his own judgment as to his sphere of activities. As a result he took it upon himself to go in search of some locomotives which had been hidden by the Mexicans. Should an invasion be attempted, they would be invaluable.

Since he was acting as an observer, MacArthur did not inform General Funston, who, in view of his instructions, would not have permitted him to go.

A reward in gold, payable upon MacArthur's safe return, secured the services of three Mexican guides. They slipped out of Vera Cruz at dusk. On foot, by handcar, by boat, and on "borrowed" horses, they finally reached Alvadaro, some thirty miles from Vera Cruz. Three serviceable engines were found.

On their return journey they ran into trouble. Outside of Salinas they met five armed men. To escape, MacArthur was forced to shoot two of them. Near Piedra they ran into a mounted party of several men. He shot four of them and the rest fled. Three bullets pierced his clothing, but he was unhurt. Near Laguna, while on a handcar, three mounted men pursued them. They outdistanced all but one, and MacArthur was forced to shoot him . . . after getting another bullet through his shirt.

In crossing the Jamapa River the boat struck a snag and sank. One of the Mexicans had been wounded, and MacArthur had a hard time holding his head above water, but they got ashore. It was just after daybreak when they reentered the American lines . . . again unobserved.

Captain Constant Cordier recommended to General Wood that MacArthur be awarded the Medal of Honor. He called the exploit "a test of supreme courage" and the "only distinguished exploit since the landing of our Army."

Wood approved. When the Award Board met it praised his courage and initiative but, since MacArthur had not informed General Funston, it recommended against setting a precedent which might encourage similar "indiscretions."

6.

THE RAINBOW DIVISION

✄ War was in the wind. Problems of unprecedented magnitude had plunged the General Staff into a frenzy of planning. Into this turmoil stepped a new Secretary of War —Newton D. Baker.

In the Chief of Staff and his assistants, he found competent administrators. But it was a strange world, and he needed an alert, well-informed younger officer who could enlighten him on various matters. He chose Major MacArthur, who had been promoted on December 11, 1915.

In June he placed MacArthur in charge of the War Department's moribund Bureau of Information, with the added duty of Press Censor. MacArthur became the Army's immediate contact with the press.

He sought advice from experienced members of the Press Corps, and his tact and sincerity went far toward enlisting their aid in preparing public opinion to accept the Selective Service Act. How well this not easily impressed body appreciated his efforts was expressed in a letter to Mr. Baker. It was signed by twenty-nine Washington correspondents, who cited the "unfailing kindness, patience, and wise counsel" with which MacArthur had discharged his duties.

The letter pleased Mr. Baker. But MacArthur was concerned with another problem. There was a war on, and he intended to get into it.

Major General William A. Mann proposed that National Guard divisions be formed and sent to France. Others opposed placing so much reliance on non-Regulars. MacArthur had faith in citizen soldiery. They had done splendid work under his father.

After forming such divisions, many states would have excess units. MacArthur suggested to Mr. Baker that a multistate division be formed from the excess. General Mann read a list of the states, from New York to California, from which the units could be drawn.

"Fine!" MacArthur exclaimed. "It will stretch over the whole country like a rainbow!" And so the historic Rainbow Division was born . . . the Fighting 42nd.

Mr. Baker approved and placed General Mann in command, with MacArthur as his chief of staff.

On August 15, 1917, MacArthur was promoted two grades to Colonel. At Camp Mills, Long Island, he and his assistants worked feverishly to organize the division and to prepare it for shipment overseas.

The twenty-seven thousand men of the Rainbow came

from twenty-six states and the District of Columbia. The old 3rd Iowa Infantry, which had served under Arthur MacArthur, became the 168th on the new Army List. The older 4th Alabama became the 167th. The still older 69th New York became the 165th—"The Fighting Irish." Cooper D. Winn's 151st Machine Gun Battalion was part of the 1st Georgia. Truly a rainbow of colorful units from east and west.

In France they received shocking news. The Rainbow was to be used as a replacement, not as a combat division. But General Pershing was not aware of Mr. Baker's love for the Rainbow. MacArthur was. Then, too, the Rainbow colonels were men of influence. Cables reached Washington, and Pershing was instructed to leave the Rainbow intact. Neither he nor certain members of his staff—"The Chaumont Crowd" —ever forgave MacArthur.

In December, Major General Charles T. Menoher relieved General Mann, who was too old for combat. In February, 1918, the Rainbow moved into a sector of the French front, east of Baccarat, for training. Aggressive raids on the German trenches drew praise from the French VI Corps commander. In a General Order, he expressed his gratitude "to the distinguished commander . . . and to his Staff so brilliantly directed by Colonel MacArthur."

Here the men of the Rainbow got to know Douglas MacArthur. He believed that a leader should be with his men. To inspire their confidence, he must be seen.

He made himself easily recognizable. He wore a black, turtleneck sweater and a short, Mackinaw type overcoat. By removing the wire from his service cap, he made a distinctive headgear which every man in the Rainbow came to recognize. He never wore a steel helmet or carried a gas mask. His only weapon was a riding crop.

Visitors from the rear echelons sometimes sneered that he was a show-off, but no one ever questioned his courage. Later General Menoher would say that "on the field of battle, where acts of heroism and valor were commonplace, his were outstanding."

On February 26, MacArthur won his first combat medal, the first of many. On a trench raid which he accompanied, there was hand-to-hand fighting. General DeBazelaire was so impressed with MacArthur's conduct that he awarded him the Croix de Guerre.

On March 9, he accompanied a French-American daylight raid to capture prisoners. His daring leadership won him the Distinguished Service Cross.

A few days later he was badly gassed. Again he refused to leave the front. "An officer's place is with his men," he insisted.

On July 4 the Rainbow marched for the Marne to participate in the tide-turning defeat of the last great German offensive of the war—the Champagne-Marne "Peace Assault." In searing heat the Rainbow dug in on the glaring, white chalk plains to await the blow. Prisoners revealed that it would fall at midnight on July 14—France's cherished Bastille Day.

When it fell, the sky seemed to be ripped apart by one vast sheet of flame as the massed guns opened fire. But the German infantry was rolled back in a shattering defeat. The Rainbow had won its spurs.

MacArthur's conduct during the battle led tough, one-armed General Gouraud to say, "I consider General MacArthur to be one of the finest and bravest soldiers I have ever served with." On July 26 MacArthur had been promoted to Brigadier General. For the time being he continued as Chief of Staff.

The Rainbow had little rest. In the terrible battles on the Ourcq, it lost 5,529 in killed and wounded during five desperate days. Many died uselessly. Sure that the Germans were in flight, higher headquarters had ordered an advance without first ascertaining the facts. The Rainbow had been decimated by the artillery and machine guns of the "fleeing" Germans. In his anguish over the senseless loss, General MacArthur vowed that he would never be guilty of committing men to battle without painstaking planning and preparation.

During the fighting an aide became alarmed at the recklessness with which MacArthur exposed himself to enemy fire.

"Sir," he implored, "you must take cover. It would be a calamity if you were killed."

"Son," MacArthur replied, "I appreciate your attitude, but the finest thing that could happen to the morale of the troops would be to have a general officer killed in action."

Before dawn on August 2 he was told that the Germans were retreating. A personal reconnaissance convinced him. There was no time to secure General Menoher's approval. By dawn MacArthur had ordered every battalion forward to harass the retreat. Had he been wrong, he would have been in jeopardy. But he was not.

His quick thinking, and his courage in assuming the responsibility, won him an Oak Leaf Cluster to his Distinguished Service Cross.

On August 6 he was assigned to command the 84th Brigade—the Iowans, Alabamians, and Georgians. At last he was in his true element. In the advance which reduced the mighty St. Mihiel salient, his men drove ahead so rapidly that he was ordered to halt and dig in.

His coolness under fire bothered members of his staff. Although he seemed to consider close shaves as routine events, they did not. Near Pannes a shell struck a farmhouse in which they were taking lunch. Several rose to dash outside, but MacArthur was unmoved.

Like Lee and Sherman, he appeared to find the battlefield stimulating. He could not remain behind an active battle front. He must go forward.

Although he was a strict disciplinarian, and demanded the utmost in bravery and endurance, the men of the 84th Brigade wanted no other leader. He slept where they slept, ate what they ate, and shared every danger. He knew every man and every man knew him. He was a "soldier's General."

The late playwright, Charles MacArthur (no relation), who served in the Rainbow, called him, "Our hell-to-breakfast brigadier, a baby who can spit nickels and chase Germans as well as any doughboy."

There were sneers from high places. Former seniors resented his higher rank and greater deeds. Some of them dubbed him the "D'Artagnan of the A.E.F.," the "Beau Brummel of the Rainbow," and less polite things; but a correspondent, commenting upon MacArthur's sartorial idiosyncracies, wrote, "You could tell he was a soldier, even in a fur coat or a bathing suit."

He visited every trench, every listening post. He knew how his men fared, and he did his best to keep them fed and clothed. As a result the morale in the 84th Brigade was as high as any in the Army. If the General could take it, so could they.

Those who saw him frequently, and came to recognize the warm humanity underlying his exterior formality, were devoted to him. But, with others, he was more respected than "liked" in the popular sense. He preferred it. Respect meant obedience . . . and fewer casualties.

On October 1 the Rainbow marched north to take part in the Meuse-Argonne offensive. On the 12th it relieved the 1st Division in front of the Côte de Chatillon, a key defense of the Hindenburg Line. Its maze of hidden cannon and machine guns had shattered the assaults of the 1st Division, which had to be withdrawn.

Alone, MacArthur went forward and inspected the ground in front of his brigade. Returning, he was caught in a cloud of poison gas. This wound was more dangerous than the first one, but again he refused to leave the front.

The 1st Division had made frontal assaults. He had a different plan. Aerial photos had revealed a gap in the German wire, through which their forward machine guns were supplied. His inspection had shown him a way to outflank those guns and to use the gap.

General Summerall, the V Corps commander, was skeptical.

"What is your estimate of your chances?" he asked.

"If we fail," MacArthur replied, "you will receive a casualty report with six thousand names, and my name will head it."

Deeply moved, Summerall gave his approval.

On the 14th and 15th parties from MacArthur's flank battalions worked through small folds in the ground until they were past the first obstacles—the forward machine guns. Silently they closed in and killed the gunners with the bayonet. On the right the Iowans seized two vantage points. Alabamians crept through the gap in the wire and joined them. Deadly fighting marked their progress; but by evening the Iowans and Alabamians were in position to smash the German left. MacArthur was ready.

At dawn on the 16th these battalions attacked the Côte de Chatillon, focusing the Germans' attentions on their threatened left. On schedule MacArthur's main attack was launched, preceded by a smashing artillery concentration and under superbly delivered machine-gun fire by Cooper Winn's Georgians.

Attacked on front and flank, and smothered by the concentrated fire, the defenses crumbled. There was fierce hand-to-hand fighting, but before evening the 84th Brigade had routed a beaten enemy. Suffering intensely from his gas wound, MacArthur reported his success from the former German command post on the Côte de Chatillon.

The Rainbow spent the last days of the war fighting its cold and weary way toward the great rail center of Sedan. By the night of November 6 it had almost reached it. His troops poised to drive on the city next morning, MacArthur lay down for a few hours' sleep. Shortly after midnight he was awakened by his adjutant.

Historically Sedan was a coveted prize. Always prestige-conscious, the Regular Army was eager to enter it first . . . to precede any National Guard division. Yet the Rainbow was almost there. A loosely written order permitted the 1st Division to ignore division boundaries and make a forced march through the Rainbow's zone. Angry confusion resulted.

MacArthur was alarmed. Unwarned, his own troops might mistake the trespassers for Germans who had infiltrated their lines. Quickly he set out with his adjutant to alert the various units.

Dawn was breaking when the job was done. Suddenly they were surrounded by a 1st Division patrol with leveled bayonets. MacArthur's cap had led them to mistake him for a German in disguise. Later he learned that only their eagerness to capture prisoners saved him from being shot.

Fortunately a Rainbow patrol arrived to identify him, and he hurried off to help untangle the confusion. He had won the distinction of being the only A.E.F. general officer to be captured by Americans.

In a few days the Armistice was signed and the Rainbow settled into snug billets along the Rhine. MacArthur assumed command.

For his courageous achievement in capturing the Côte de Chatillon, General Menoher had recommended that MacArthur be awarded the Medal of Honor. Instead, he was awarded a second Oak Leaf Cluster to his Distinguished Service Cross. Again his country's highest award for valor had been denied him.

A letter from General Pershing eased the disappointment.

"It gives me great pleasure," the General wrote, "to inform you that on Oct. 17, I recommended you for promotion to the grade of Major General. . . ."

The signing of the Armistice stopped all promotions to high grades, but his services had been recognized by the Commander-in-Chief.

Other superiors also recorded their high regard for his services. Several of the Allied governments awarded him decorations. When he left France, Douglas MacArthur had been wounded twice, decorated thirteen times, and cited seven times for bravery.

7.

CHIEF OF STAFF

✕ In the opinion of General Peyton C. March, Chief of Staff, West Point was "forty years behind the times." Its curriculum was antiquated. To meet wartime demands, three classes had been graduated during 1918, stripping the Corps of Cadets of upper class leadership. March selected MacArthur to bring West Point up to date, and to improve its academic standards.

A hidebound Academic Board tried to obstruct his plans to enrich the curriculum. Powerful pacifists strove to abolish the school. An economy-minded Congress favored a three-year course.

For three years MacArthur fought and pleaded. Finally the full course was restored and the curriculum was broadened until he was satisfied that it would prepare graduates "for the next war, not the last one." But he had made powerful enemies.

MacArthur made many changes. Physical fitness was stressed, and participation in intramural athletics became mandatory. Tennis and other games were permitted on Sunday. When church groups protested, he insisted that it was better to "get the cadets out of their rooms and under the blue sky." The morale of the cadets rose, and the rise was reflected in their grades.

Hazing and the harsh bullying of plebes were traditional. He abolished hazing, and changed the indoctrination of plebes to a stern but dignified preceptorship. Old Grads, schooled in the harsh tradition, railed that he was ruining the Corps.

MacArthur was strict but, remembering his own cadet days, he knew when to overlook infractions.

On February 28, 1920, he was appointed a Brigadier General in the Regular Army. The fact that he had been singled out to retain his wartime rank was deeply resented by many of the officers who had already reverted to peacetime rank. But Secretary Baker felt that the nation would have too great a need for MacArthur's obvious talents to bury them in an inarticulate grade. He had called him "our greatest front-line commander."

When the Prince of Wales visited West Point, MacArthur ignored precedent. Rather than subject the young prince to a boring round of inspection and parade, he chose four outstanding cadets to take charge of him. While MacArthur entertained the Prince's entourage, the cadets gave Edward a relaxed and memorable day.

On February 14, 1922, MacArthur was married to Mrs. Louise Cromwell Brooks in a fashionable ceremony at the Palm Beach villa of the bride's stepfather, financier Edward Stotesbury.

It was not destined to be a happy union. She loved the excitement of her gay social world. By nature, he was a recluse. They shared no common interest.

A few days later he was assigned to the Philippines. His job at West Point was done. He had not seen the islands since 1904, and he was eager to return.

In October the MacArthurs reached Manila. He renewed old friendships and made new friends, among them the rising Filipino leader, Manuel Quezon. Distressed at the tendency of the American colony, civilian and military, to treat the native Filipinos as a lesser people, he strove by conspicuous example to gain their complete social acceptance. His efforts were resented by the whole foreign colony, but they won him the lasting confidence of the Filipino people.

On January 17, 1925, he was promoted to Major General. A few days later the MacArthurs sailed for home. He departed reluctantly, but she was eager to go. She had found the climate enervating and Manila society boring.

He was stationed first in Atlanta and then in Baltimore. In October he was detailed to serve on the General Court Martial convened to try Brigadier General "Billy" Mitchell on charges of insubordination. Mitchell's zeal in crusading for greater air power had led him to overstep lawful bounds.

In Milwaukee, for three generations, the MacArthurs and the Mitchells had been friends. MacArthur was reluctant to sit in judgment of his boyhood companion, but the duty could not be avoided.

It was an unusual trial. Regardless of his reasons, Mitchell had attacked his superior officers publicly. The Articles of War were explicit. The prosecution presented its case and rested.

The defense was permitted wide latitude. For four weeks it tried to shift the issue away from the charge and to the case for air power. Brilliant witnesses were presented. Their testimony was a revelation, and MacArthur gained a conception of potential air strength that would serve the country well later on.

But the real issue before the court was clear, and the evidence conclusive. Mitchell was found guilty and suspended from command. He preferred to resign.

For years MacArthur would be attacked for his part in the Mitchell trial. There was no persecution. The discipline and good order of the Army simply could not be subordinated to any one man's opinions, no matter how brilliant or how constructive.

Many believe that MacArthur voted for acquittal . . . and that he blocked a sentence of dismissal. It is not unlikely. He sympathized with Mitchell's zeal, even though he deplored his bad judgment. He believed in an officer's right to air his honest beliefs. But court members are sworn to secrecy. He has never disclosed his vote.

In September, 1927, he became president of the American Olympic Committee and assumed the involved task of preparing the American participation in the coming games. The record proves his success. In Amsterdam the following June, the American team won first place with 131 points. Finland, their nearest rival, won 62.

Again he was assigned to Manila, this time to command

the entire Philippine Department. His wife did not accompany him. During his absence she won an uncontested divorce. It was not done in anger. She could not conform to his pattern of life, nor he to hers. A Manila editor offered to kill the story. MacArthur thanked him but refused the special privilege.

Grimly he watched the growing might of Japan, while at home the pacifists were gnawing away at the country's defenses. He was eager to combat the inroads of Communism.

On August 15, 1930, he was notified that he would succeed General Summerall as Chief of Staff. On October 30, in Washington, he was sworn in and donned the four stars of a General. He had reached the top.

Immediately he faced trouble. Prominent clergymen sought to abolish the armed forces—to rely upon brotherly love to turn away foreign wrath. Under their moral suasion, 62 percent of the Protestant clergy voted that American churches should not support any future wars.

To the press, MacArthur pointed out that those ministers had, in effect, proclaimed "their willingness to see this country perish rather than to participate in its defense." His words did not halt the pacifists, but they made many ministers think.

In September, 1931, MacArthur attended the French Army maneuvers as the guest of General Weygand, French Chief of Staff. At their close he was decorated with the Grand Cross of the Legion of Honor.

In June of 1932 the Bonus Marchers began arriving in Washington to demand immediate payment of a bonus for World War I service. Led by Walter W. Waters, most of them were bona-fide veterans who felt that they had a just claim. They set up temporary camps on Anacostia Flats, within the city.

Posing as veterans, many toughs, panhandlers, and sneak thieves prowled the city, angering the citizens and taxing the resources of the police. The situation was made to order for Communist exploitation, and they quickly moved in.

Chief of Police Pelham D. Glassford soon had ample evidence that the Communists had arrived and were in full control. Although he had persuaded large numbers of the veterans to accept train tickets and return home, about five thousand of the more reckless ones remained.

After an abortive attempt by the outnumbered police to clear the city and restore order, during which one marcher was killed, the commissioners appealed to President Hoover. Immediately MacArthur was directed to oust the men.

Earlier he had advised the city officials against the use of force. Since some six thousand veterans had already gone home, he believed that, with patience, the rest could be dispersed peacefully. The Communists could be arrested and dealt with later, not as leaders of a formidable mob. Now it was too late. Waters, who had promised to cooperate, had been ousted by the Communists when they seized control.

Quickly troops were assembled—infantry, cavalry, tanks—about seven hundred in all. MacArthur sent to his quarters for a uniform. It was the usual duty uniform, with his service ribbons on the left breast. He changed from civilian clothes in his office.

The troops moved steadily through the streets and cleared the area. Not a shot was fired and no unnecessary force was used. The mere sight of fixed bayonets, and of the cavalry and tanks, had done most of the work. It was an unpleasant task, but it was completely successful.

Months later a bedraggled unfortunate asked to see Mac-Arthur. Upon his assertion that he was an old soldier, he was admitted. MacArthur, like William Tecumseh Sherman, never turned aside an old soldier. It was Waters. MacArthur fed him and found him a job.

The "Victory at Anacostia Flats" proved to be a dear one for MacArthur. From coast to coast the press lampooned the "Four Star General on Horseback," who had evicted "hungry women and children at the point of the bayonet." The "Prussian cruelty" with which he had "broken the heads of hungry men" was a "wanton disgrace to a civilized people."

"Mr. Hoover's popinjay chief of staff" was excoriated by experts in the art of smearing. He was assailed the most bitterly by Drew Pearson and in the *Daily Worker*. His "prancing white horse" and his "medal-bedecked full-dress uniform" became familiar to the public, even though neither existed. Even his World War I record was subjected to sneers and distortions, and the appellation "Dugout Doug" was created by hostile columnists.

Stung though he must have been, he offered no explanations ... made no defense. Faced with an unpleasant duty, he had discharged it without "passing the buck," as he might easily have done.

His years as Chief of Staff were unprecedentedly difficult. All through the 1920's the Army had fought a losing battle with pacifism, Congressional hostility, and an apathetic public. Our defenses had fallen into a state of impotence comparable to those of a bankrupt banana republic. The mighty American Army, which had broken the Hindenburg Line and saved the Allies from disaster, had been reduced to a widely scattered police force. There was increasing pressure to do away with it altogether. There would be no more wars!

If ever his voice was raised in persuasive eloquence, it was through those years. He pleaded—sometimes, he felt, almost abjectly—for a strong air force, for improved arms, for motorization, and for a modern tank force. Little by little he made headway.

Fortunately MacArthur won the support of a man who could sense the hostilities astir in the world—Franklin Delano Roosevelt, who had succeeded President Hoover in 1933. They were old friends, distant cousins, and amazingly alike. Yet MacArthur sometimes found the President opposing him.

Even though he knew that MacArthur was invariably right, Roosevelt was a politician; sometimes he had much to gain by heeding an economy-minded Congress. Matters reached a boiling point when the President agreed to discharge two thousand Regular Army officers. Angry words aroused both men. Finally MacArthur rose from his chair and bowed with cold formality.

"Mr. President," he warned, "your policy will destroy the American Army. You leave me no choice. I must resign from the Army and carry this fight to the American people." He saluted and left the room. Outside the nervous tension caused him to be physically ill on the immaculate White House lawn.

The President was enraged. Not even Rexford Tugwell or Harry Hopkins could talk to him like that. But, as his anger cooled, his patriotism won out over his political instincts. He vetoed the proposed army cuts. Further, he allocated large amounts of relief funds to modernize the Army.

To MacArthur's untiring efforts could be credited two other vital gains—a General Headquarters Air Force, which provided immediate striking power, and the Four Army Plan, a speedy means of mobilizing the country for war.

He was the Army's most effective speaker. His feeling for words, his sense of timing, and the intensity with which he could hold attention sometimes made his extemporaneous speeches so dramatic that reporters poked fun at his "ten-dollar words" and "million-dollar mannerisms."

If his dramatic effects were deliberate, and if words and phrases were chosen for sentimental effect, they served their purpose. He was praised and applauded, ridiculed and damned, but he was never ignored. For underneath any stage dressing of gesture or rhetoric, his statements made unshakeable good sense—and he was usually right. Like Churchill—another distant cousin—he knew how to be heard.

In the press and from pacifist pulpits, MacArthur was subjected to vicious attacks. Most of them were borne in silence; but the continued jibes and innuendoes of Drew Pearson decided him to enter suit for libel. Damages of $1,750,000 were asked. Suddenly MacArthur withdrew his suit and paid the court costs.

Later a retired officer, who had known him through the years, said that "although he has always been spattered with mud, there is nothing about Douglas MacArthur for it to cling to. He keeps himself too clean." Yet, like all unique people, he was often the object of the slander and vituperation of complete strangers.

Two unfortunate matters hardened George Catlett Marshall's resentment of MacArthur into bitter enmity. Neither was MacArthur's fault.

In 1933 General Pershing asked him to have Marshall made a Brigadier General. Although Marshall lacked the requisite seniority as a Colonel, MacArthur sent his name to the Selection Board.

Unfortunately an inspector had just found Marshall's command deficient and had made an adverse report. Considering both factors, the Board did not select him. Nevertheless, Marshall blamed MacArthur for not pushing the promotion through despite the Board.

Later MacArthur was directed to send "the best officer available" to Chicago to direct the training of the Illinois National Guard. MacArthur asked the Chief of Infantry for his recommendation.

"I would send George Marshall," he was told.

Marshall, who preferred duty with troops, was sent. He never forgave MacArthur.

Yet neither matter was detrimental to Marshall. In Chicago he made valuable contacts. And the adverse inspection report had stemmed largely from his preoccupation with the many Civilian Conservation Corps camps for which he was responsible, in addition to his military command. This interest led to acquaintance with Harry Hopkins and others high in President Roosevelt's favor. After a while he was said to be one of this circle.

When MacArthur's four-year tour as Chief of Staff was over, the President broke precedent by appointing him for another year. They sometimes clashed, but Roosevelt had confidence in him.

"I must always find a way to keep Douglas close to me," he told intimates. "If we have another A.E.F., he's the man to take it over."

During that year MacArthur began to wonder about his future. He was already at the top. Any usual assignment would be subordinate to his present post. Then a new field opened.

In 1934 Congress had passed the Tydings-McDuffie Act, under which the Philippines would receive full independence in 1946. In the meantime they would assume Commonwealth status. Until 1946 the United States would continue to be responsible for their defense. But after that?

Manuel Quezon visited Washington. In November he would become President of the new Commonwealth. Tormented by the problem of his country's future security, he called on MacArthur. "Could the islands be defended by Filipino forces after 1946?" he asked.

"I *know* they can," MacArthur reassured him. It would take time and money, he explained, but it could be done.

It would be a task for a strong man—a man of great military reputation, and one whom the people of the Philippines had already learned to trust. Only MacArthur fitted the role.

When Quezon asked that MacArthur be loaned to the Commonwealth government to create its defense force, Roosevelt approved. It was agreed that he would remain for six years. Quezon's spirits soared. In September, Roosevelt asked MacArthur if he would like to be the first High Commissioner to the Philippine Commonwealth. MacArthur was honored, but he could not leave the Army. Then, too, he had pledged his word to Quezon.

En route to Manila, Mary MacArthur began to fail. She was in her eighty-fourth year, but her son would not leave her behind. He spent almost all of his time by her side, but on one of his turns around the deck in the open air he was introduced to a slender, attractive young lady from Tennessee—Miss Jean Faircloth. By the time the ship reached Manila they had become closely acquainted, so much so that she decided to stay on in Manila for a while. She was destined to remain for a long time.

In December, Mary MacArthur died. In February her son accompanied her remains to Washington. She was buried in Arlington National Cemetery, beside her husband.

MacArthur hurried back to Manila and plunged into the challenging task of making any attempt to invade the Philippines a costly undertaking. He had ten years—so he thought—in which to create a self-sustaining Philippine Army.

8.

AN UNPRECEDENTED RANK

✗ As Military Adviser to the Philippine Commonwealth government, MacArthur drafted a National Defense Act for the Commonwealth Assembly. It provided for a small regular Army of 350 officers and five thousand enlisted men. Its mission was to train the reserve divisions upon which the defense of the Philippines would rely.

By 1946 some four hundred thousand Filipinos would be trained and ready to defend their homeland. They would be organized into forty divisions, each to be organized in the home area of its personnel. In this defense army modeled on the Swiss system, every male citizen would be ready to serve his country at a designated place.

Although the Filipinos are natural fighters, many Americans doubted if they would accept the disciplined life of soldiers. To their lasting credit, they did . . . and vied with each other in working to achieve professional dependability.

A Military Academy was established at Baguio. It was staffed largely by Filipino graduates of West Point—enough to model the new school after the proud tenets of the old. Inspired by pride and a sense of honor, Moslem and Christian were welded into a corps whose morale, discipline, and academic standards were soon on a par with fine academies everywhere.

Army officers questioned both the dependability of the Filipinos and the actual defensibility of the islands. MacArthur believed firmly in both, provided that all conditions had been met—in money and in time. It was not that he believed that the islands could be made impregnable by Philippine resources alone. But he believed that, once his plans were fulfilled, not even the Japanese would waste the manpower and the matériel necessary to gain a secure foothold.

"By 1946," he prophesied, "I shall have made of these islands a Pacific Switzerland which will cost any invader five hundred thousand men, three years of labor, and five billion dollars to conquer. And no invader will be given three years!"

One man was delighted with his progress—Manuel Quezon. On August 24, 1936, he took an unprecedented step. He bestowed upon a somewhat embarrassed MacArthur the rank of Field Marshal in the Army of the Philippine Commonwealth.

It was then that "the cap" came into being . . . the cap which has been so widely described as "gaudy," as "gold-braided," and as a MacArthur vanity. In a sense it was, as one writer put it, a "MacArthur creation." In selecting a service cap different from that of the United States Army, he merely had the decades-old blue dress cap of the American uniform reproduced in khaki.

The cap became his trade-mark. It would become an affront to anti-MacArthur journalists; but to the Filipinos, and later to the South Koreans, it would become a symbol of liberation and victory.

The Army grew, but MacArthur faced many problems. The annual appropriation which Quezon had promised had been reduced. Powerful Filipino politicians had discovered the pocket-lining opportunities in "public works," and were diverting defense money to these ends. To ease the threat of a war in Manchuria, the Russians—who had made powerful friends in Washington—schemed to keep the Philippines defenseless . . . and the way open for the Japanese to move south, away from Manchuria. Business interests fought against Philippine independence and the end of duty-free imports.

The Japanese worked to undermine Filipino faith in Mac-Arthur, and to assure the Filipino government that it was MacArthur's presence alone that threatened the peace.

"Remove him and our friendly relations will remain undisturbed," they urged.

Through it all MacArthur's faith gave impetus to his plan.

Miss Faircloth's visit had become a lengthy one. Most of the General's free time was spent with her. Although younger bachelors competed for her interest, they received little more than pleasant smiles.

In February of 1937 Quezon journeyed to Washington to discuss the Commonwealth's economic future with officials and financiers. With him, he took his military adviser and close confidant, MacArthur. Miss Faircloth left the islands at the same time by plane.

In Washington, MacArthur took a short leave from Quezon. On Friday morning, April 30, he met Miss Faircloth in New York. At ten o'clock, they were married in a civil ceremony at the Municipal Building. Two of his staff accompanied him. She had no attendants. It had been a well-kept secret.

Back in Washington, he found that he had become an outsider. It was rumored that George Marshall, who had become Brigadier at Pershing's insistence, was the man to watch. Marshall had become an ardent New Dealer and had captured the President's fancy. MacArthur found, too, that events in Europe had turned the President's eyes in that direction. Hitler was becoming a force to reckon with . . . much more so, in Washington eyes, than the Japanese.

In Manila the MacArthurs lived in a large, air-conditioned apartment atop the Manila Hotel. Their entertaining was limited to close friends, and to a few visiting notables and resident dignitaries. If any of the latter were not, in MacArthur's eyes, above reproach, it was unlikely that they would ever see the great mahogany table in the MacArthur dining room, or the fine old silver which graced it. Rank and position were not enough.

There was a touch of tender but old-fashioned formality in Mrs. MacArthur's way of addressing her husband. If she ever called him "Douglas," it was in private. In the manner of her forebears, she called him "General." And he, as unfailingly courteous, responded usually with "Ma'am?"

In August he received shocking news. The six-year tour of

duty to which President Roosevelt had agreed was being reduced to two. He was to be ordered home.

Sadly he chose the only alternative. On December 31, 1937, he was placed on the Retired List at his own request. And even though he had been assured that he would be retired in the grade of General, on the retirement order he was shown as a Major General.

The new army was growing slowly, but there were discouragements. Although he had begun to receive additional officers to assist in the training, they were far from enough. There was a dearth of supplies. Yet loyal friends aided him, sometimes at great risk.

Under the Five Power Naval Treaty of 1922, Japan and America had agreed not to fortify Pacific holdings. To the Japanese it was a joke, but MacArthur's hands were tied.

On Corregidor the large coast defense guns had been outranged by Japan's battleships. By moving them to higher sites, their range could be increased. The State Department refused to permit it.

Corregidor was commanded by a brave and resolute man, Brigadier General Walter K. Wilson. He took a grave personal risk. He turned his head, as it were, while MacArthur, with Filipino labor, got the job done.

Had the secret leaked out, he would have been dealt with severely. But the resighted guns of Corregidor later kept the Japanese fleet from flanking the defenders of Bataan. And the defense of Bataan ruined the Japanese timetable and saved Australia from invasion. Walter King Wilson was one of the unsung heroes of World War II.

Despite such acts of loyalty by dedicated colleagues, Mac-

Arthur still faced obstructionism. Stung by the writings of a newspaper analyst, he blazed forth:

"These islands must and will be defended. I am here by the grace of God. This is my destiny!"

On February 21, 1938, his wife bore him a son. It was the fulfillment of a dream. Again there was an Arthur MacArthur to perpetuate the name. For the moment his cares were forgotten in the pride of parenthood.

In Europe the war clouds grew darker. On September 1, 1939, Hitler smashed into Poland and a fresh holocaust was in the making. On the same day George Marshall was appointed Chief of Staff. The sponsorship of Harry Hopkins and others close to the President had caused him to be promoted over the heads of every senior Brigadier and Major General in the Army.

America was preparing for war, but MacArthur was not aware that, when it came, the Atlantic would be considered the vital theater, the Pacific a secondary one. But he knew that supplies were flowing to England in vast quantities, and few to the Philippines. On June 22, 1941, when Hitler attacked Russia, supplies began to flow also to that doubtful ally. The Philippines were ignored, and MacArthur began to feel that he was forgotten.

One man had not forgotten him—the President. He had, in fact, kept himself very well informed as to MacArthur's progress. And then one day—July 26, 1941—he startled both official Washington and the Pacific world by recalling MacArthur to active duty as Commanding General, U. S. Army Forces in the Far East—USAFFE—with the rank of Lieutenant General. Another Presidential Order mobilized the Philippine Army under his command.

If these acts created consternation among those in Washington who thought themselves rid of him for all time, they created confidence in Asia. French, British, Dutch, Australians—from Hanoi to Singapore and from Java to Australia—all on the Japanese timetable, felt a new surge of hope. They knew MacArthur. He would fight.

To the Japanese, it meant that the man whom they held to be America's ablest commander would be their immediate antagonist. Time, however, was in their favor. They were ready and he was not. They must strike before he could fully prepare.

MacArthur's plans had not reached the halfway mark toward completion, but if war was delayed until spring he would have more than 120,000 Filipinos trained and armed —with World War I weapons. And he was confident that he would be sent trained troops from the busy training camps which had sprung up at home.

He requested troops, modern arms and trained officers for his Filipino regiments, competent specialists, tanks, radar equipment, and adequate air forces. Few of his requests were granted. An antiaircraft regiment arrived, a tank battalion, and a maintenance company. Their equipment was outdated.

In the War Department dedicated staff officers tried to meet his needs, but many of his most urgent requests were denied by General Marshall. When the War Plans Division recommended that all American forces in the Philippine area —Army and Navy—be unified under MacArthur's command, he pigeonholed it.

Earlier MacArthur had made a recommendation that would change the whole concept of the military role of the

Philippines from one of defense to one of offense. By basing heavy bombers, strongly supported by dive bombers and fighter craft, in widely dispersed fields, Japan's invasion route could be interdicted and Japan itself threatened with retaliation if an invasion of the Philippines was attempted.

It came to the attention of the President and General Arnold, Chief of the Air Corps, and won their approval. In October, 1941, the first few B-17's reached Clark Field, sixty-four miles north of Manila. They were followed by fifty crated P-40E fighter planes and a complement of Air Corps personnel. They were "too little and too late." And even though in September other items had begun to flow toward the islands in greater quantities, they too were not sent soon enough—and there were not enough of them.

Early in October Major General Lewis H. Brereton had been selected to command the new air forces in the Philippines. A tough, realistic officer, he questioned the advisability of sending the B-17's before they could be protected, and before adequate bases had been prepared. And he questioned the realism of official Washington's tentative date for the possible beginning of a Japanese attack—April 1, 1942.

Relations between the two countries continued to deteriorate. In Japan, Hideki Tojo became Premier. Tojo was uncompromisingly determined upon war.

The Philippines, accorded lower priority than embattled Europe, became the object of alarmed concern. Dates of projected troop shipments were advanced, and all classes of supplies were rushed to Pacific ports. It was of no avail. War came too quickly.

From Manila, MacArthur watched the Japanese. For public consumption, he adhered to the Washington estimate of

April 1 as the earliest date upon which war might begin. Privately he and his staff worked feverishly to prepare for what might occur any day. Every unit was alerted; every disposition made; every precaution taken.

As a final measure, he ordered the 35 B-17 Flying Fortress bombers, which had arrived at Clark Field, flown to Del Monte Field, on Mindanao, some five hundred miles south. All he could do now was watch and wait.

9.

"I SHALL RETURN"

✗   At 3:40 A.M., December 8, Manila time, MacArthur was awakened by the telephone.

"Jap planes are attacking Pearl Harbor!" he was told.

"Pearl Harbor! That should be our strongest point!" In a few minutes he was at his headquarters.

At nine-thirty a large force of Japanese bombers crossed Lingayen Gulf, flying toward Manila. Fighters took off to intercept them, but they changed course and bombed the summer capital at Baguio.

Seventeen B-17's had not been moved to Del Monte Field. These were sent aloft as a safety measure.

When the all-clear sounded, the fighters were recalled to Clark Field. Although the B-17's could have remained aloft for several hours, safe from destruction on the ground, they, too, were recalled. While the crews took lunch, all ships were gassed. Then the enemy struck again.

Within minutes fifteen of the B-17's were destroyed. The two others were seriously damaged. It was a shocking loss. And Clark Field, the only fully equipped field in the islands, was a wreck.

MacArthur heard the news sadly but he uttered no word of censure, despite the fact that his orders to remove the planes to safety had not been obeyed. Later it was claimed that MacArthur's refusal to authorize a bombing raid on Formosa caused the disaster, that the planes would have been in the air. MacArthur was bound by orders. Then, too, the planes had been in the air—until they were ordered in for lunch.

The Japanese moved swiftly. Landings were made at distant points to lure MacArthur into dividing his forces. He ignored them and waited for their main effort, which he believed would be at Lingayen Gulf. The enemy timetable was fixed. In a matter of days General Masaharu Homma's powerful forces would crush American and Filipino resistance. Then most of them could be withdrawn for use in New Guinea or the Solomon Islands, preparatory to invading Australia.

It was expected that MacArthur would make an all-out effort to hold Manila. It would be a forlorn hope. Once Manila was taken, the Japanese believed that Filipino resistance would cease. If the American units managed to escape into the Bataan Peninsula, they would soon be hunted down and destroyed.

The Japanese failed to recognize two factors—the determination of the Filipinos, and the care with which MacArthur had planned to thwart the Japanese. These were their undoing. The protracted defense of Bataan became a decisive factor in their ultimate defeat.

Immediately MacArthur disrupted Japanese plans by evacuating Manila. Skillfully he withdrew his main forces—Wainwright's I Corps from Lingayen, where it had delayed Japanese landings, and Jones's II Corps from south of Manila—into the thick jungles of mountainous Bataan.

Cavalry, in a historical curtain call, destroyed bridges, cut off advance parties, and laid traps for Japanese tanks.

MacArthur's total force numbered not more than eighty thousand; Homma's nearly two hundred thousand. About fifty thousand of the defenders were Filipinos, poorly armed, poorly equipped, half-trained, and with inexperienced officers. There was little artillery, few tanks, and no reserves of foods or medicines.

On December 18 MacArthur was promoted for a second time to the rank of full General. He was too busy for rejoicing.

On the 24th he informed President Quezon that the government must move to Corregidor. At midnight the Quezons, High Commissioner Sayre and his family, the MacArthurs, and various others boarded a small steamer for the trip across Manila Bay. It was Christmas Eve.

Earlier Jean MacArthur had packed clothing and other necessities for each member of the family—the General, herself, little Arthur and his old Chinese amah, who had tended him almost from birth. At the last moment she took a dress from her bag to make room for more precious things—the medals which had been awarded to the General through the years. In his bag she had already packed pictures of his father and his mother. Everything else was left behind.

On the 26th Corregidor received its first heavy air attack.

MacArthur took up quarters in a frame house on lower Corregidor, exposed to attacks from the air. During air raids his family sought a nearby shelter, but he preferred to watch the progress and note the damage.

Once his Filipino orderly clapped his own helmet on MacArthur's head when a bomb dropped close by them. MacArthur calmly replaced it on the orderly's head. As he did so a bomb fragment struck it, but MacArthur went on watching the raid.

On the 27th MacArthur declared Manila an "open city," but the Japanese continued to bomb it until their forces had entered the city.

On Bataan the lines extended from the China Sea to Manila Bay, almost in the area where Aguinaldo had defied General Arthur MacArthur. It was difficult country. The central area was mountainous. Thick jungles enabled attacking groups to approach under cover until ready to launch a bloody "banzai" charge. But the embattled Filamerican forces dug in and stemmed the Japanese tide.

On January 2 the Japanese entered Manila unopposed, but the great guns of Corregidor kept Japanese ships at a distance. Admiral Hart's small Far East squadron slipped out of Manila Bay to rendezvous with the English and the Dutch, far to the south. Only submarines and PT boats remained.

Its rear guarded by Corregidor, the ruggedness of Bataan offered a secure refuge so long as supplies lasted. Unfortunately these were already short, and masses of civilians had flocked into Bataan ahead of the forces. They had to be fed. Rationing became an immediate necessity.

The story of Bataan is one of glory for its defenders. Sure that relief would come—that some of the vast flow of supplies which the Russians were demanding would be diverted to them—the troops fought desperately against inexhaustible numbers.

MacArthur, in likelihood, was not yet aware that the European front had been accorded priority. As the days passed he sensed that something was wrong. Heated exchanges of messages with Washington confirmed his suspicions.

He argued that Japanese fleet units were widely dispersed to support Nippon's many invasion projects. The enemy blockade of the Philippines was, therefore, "paper thin." There would be risks; but American broadcasts told the men on Bataan of huge convoys laden with supplies braving the Nazi U-boat "wolf packs" and dive bombers to reach European ports. Why not the Philippines? they asked. Only three loaded cargo ships reached Mindanao . . . from Australia.

Neither hunger nor doubt could dispel humor. When MacArthur visited Bataan, he found a large calendar nailed to a tree; on it the picture of a full-rigged ship under sail. A new caption was scrawled above the old: "We told you so. Help is on the way."

A movement was started to "Buy a Bomber for Bataan," if one could be spared from Europe. A "special war zone bonus" was offered to the crew that delivered it. MacArthur enjoyed the irony.

In his dispatches MacArthur gave high praise to his embattled troops. He was proud that they had already become veterans. He was quick to recognize individual acts of bravery.

Dengue fever reduced the firing line. Malaria took a heavy toll. On half-rations, resistance lowered and men fell ill more quickly. The troops on Bataan were raked and pounded with artillery and machine-gun fire, and bombed continually from the air. Corregidor was battered by heavy artillery and blasted with heavy bombs. Its tunnels were jammed with sick and wounded, with families and army nurses.

In January the Quezon family, and a few others, were removed to Australia by submarine. Mrs. MacArthur chose not to go.

"We three shall stay together," she told her husband.

With a little daring, MacArthur insisted, convoys could get through. As bad as things were, however, MacArthur would probably not have survived the fall of the Philippines had not events in Australia changed his destiny.

On December 23 Prime Minister Churchill and a large retinue visited Washington to shape war policy. Among other things, it was agreed that, if necessary, even Australia would be allowed to fall until Hitler had been defeated.

The resulting blast from Australia shook even the complacent Churchill. In no uncertain terms Prime Minister John Curtin stated Australia's stand.

". . . Australia looks to America," he wrote, "free from any pangs about our traditional links of friendship with Britain. We refuse to accept the dictum that the Pacific struggle is a subordinate segment of the general conflict."

There was more to his message, but these thoughts were enough to hurry a placating message from Churchill. The

Empire was already dissolving. England could not afford to lose its angry Commonwealth "down under."

Curtin demanded—and obtained—the return of three Australian divisions which were serving England elsewhere. And the Australian Parliament requested that General MacArthur be ordered to Australia to assume command of the entire Southwest Pacific. He was.

At first MacArthur rebelled. He could not leave his troops. The impossibility of disobeying the Commander-in-Chief was pointed out. Besides, Roosevelt's message had assured him that an American force was being assembled in Australia to redeem the area of Japanese conquest. Who else, he was asked, was qualified to organize and lead it?

MacArthur withheld his decision for two days, then asked for a delay until the Filipino people could be told the reason for his departure. It was granted.

He divided the forces in the islands into separate, independent commands. It was obvious that Bataan's days were numbered; yet Mindanao—even Corregidor—might hold out indefinitely. By retaining for himself the over-all command, no single commander could surrender the whole force. If Mindanao held out, it would serve as a staging area for the forces sent to regain Luzon.

Marshall, however, announced publicly that General Jonathan M. Wainwright had taken command. Later the Japanese used this announcement to force from Wainwright an over-all surrender.

By March 11 MacArthur's plans were made. Lieutenant John D. Bulkeley, of the Navy, prepared four PT boats for the venture. Shortly after seven o'clock MacArthur left his headquarters for the last time. At their quarters his family was ready.

In the gathering darkness the party assembled on the Corregidor dock. The selection of that party had been one of MacArthur's hardest decisions. Sixteen experienced staff members, whom he would need immediately in Australia; his secretary, a trusted sergeant; himself. Three others would add little weight to the crowded boats: Mrs. MacArthur, Arthur, and his devoted amah, Ah Cheu.

Later, slanders would appear, both at home and afloat. Even today some former navy men believe that nurses were left behind to make room for the MacArthur furniture—even the grand piano. Bulkeley, who carried the MacArthur baggage aboard his boat, has stated that he "took it all in one trip."

It was a perilous journey. Chances of success were estimated at one in ten. The engines, carboned up, could not attain normal high speed. Drums of gasoline added weight. There was no shelter from the drenching spray.

On the dock MacArthur bade good-by to faithful friends—Wainwright, his classmate Paul Bunker, officers and men, American and Filipino.

To Wainwright, he said, "Hold out until I come for you. I shall return."

His words were prophetic. Immediately Colonel Carlos Romulo, a Manila editor serving on MacArthur's staff, recognized them as inspirational. Later, when MacArthur had reached Australia and restated this simple pledge, Romulo broadcast them over the Corregidor station "The Voice of Freedom." These words were both a challenge and a pledge.

Surreptitiously they appeared everywhere to reassure the people and worry the Japanese. They became the motto of the resistance government.

The boats were armed with .50-caliber machine guns. Each carried four torpedos. They were highly maneuverable. With luck they could destroy any Japanese ship that got in their way. MacArthur's orders were to attack if intercepted. If attacked from the air, they must depend upon fast evasive maneuvers and a screen of machine-gun fire.

The seas were heavy and the little boats shuddered under hammer-like blows. In the darkness they lost formation. After daybreak they rendezvoused in a small cove on an uninhabited island. Mistaking Bulkeley's boat—the last in—for a Japanese, another dumped its spare gasoline and almost opened fire before MacArthur was recognized.

Little Arthur, Ah Cheu, and some others were deathly ill. All had been painfully buffeted by the savage waves. At last Mindanao was reached. The travelers had not been seen, an argument in itself for MacArthur's contention that the blockade was "paper thin."

On Mindanao the Japanese were soon aware of their presence. Their route was obvious; so, when they approached Darwin, in B-17's sent from Australia, it was being bombed. They were advised to land at Batchellor Field, fifty miles away. The Japanese followed them. Finally they landed at Alice Springs, deep in the hot, sandy Australian bush. There the MacArthurs and several others transferred to a Melbourne-bound train. The rest proceeded by air.

All of them needed rest. Weeks had passed since they had known a full meal or more than scanty sleep. As the train crawled across the lower half of the continent, Mac-Arthur rested . . . but he also thought and planned.

Quickly he would prepare the waiting troops for the hard tasks which lay ahead. When planes had arrived, and ships were made ready, he would begin a counteroffensive which would sweep the Japanese from his path and open the road to the Philippines. Bataan would be avenged . . . perhaps even saved.

But on Bataan the defenders were dwindling in numbers and in strength. Quarter rations could sustain life, but they could not keep men fit for battle. Supplies were almost exhausted. The cavalry horses had been eaten, and caribou were being slaughtered for meat.

Clothing was in rags, and shoes were disintegrating. Sickness and wounds were taking a steadily increasing toll. Finally the end came. Although they had exacted a terrible price from the Japanese, the gaunt, starved men had simply become too weak to kill any more of them. But, to their eternal glory, they had disrupted irreparably the minutely planned Japanese scheme of conquest.

Rather than troops being withdrawn from the Philippines to complete the seizure of New Guinea and the Solomons, troops had been diverted from other invasion projects to stiffen Homma's battered army.

Almost six priceless months had been lost to them while "MacArthur's invincibles" held out. It was too late now to make Guadalcanal a fortress which would isolate Australia from the Western world. The real battle for Guadalcanal had been won on Bataan.

Neither MacArthur nor his men had failed. His Filipinos had fought with a fury that outdid even his faith in them.

Had supplies been sent through the "paper-thin" blockade, starvation and disease might not have defeated them.

When the train reached Adelaide, MacArthur's high hopes crashed into ruins. He received the crushing news that there were no American divisions in Australia, no gathering army of revenge. Only a few token units.

10.

HIT 'EM WHERE THEY AIN'T

✄ Disappointment gave way to complete astonishment when MacArthur's train reached Melbourne, and he saw the cheering crowds waiting to greet him. His spirits lifted.

A platoon of Engineers formed an honor guard. Had they been his old Rainbow troops, he could not have been more proud. He saw them as the point of a great American spear which he would thrust straight at the Japanese homeland.

In Canberra, the capital, Prime Minister Curtin welcomed him warmly. In the presence of the Australian Parliament, the American Ambassador, in the name of the President, bestowed upon him the priceless decoration which he had twice been denied—the Medal of Honor.

His first task was to revive the faith of the Australian people. In their desperation they had planned to yield three-fifths of their country to save the rest—to fight on the so-called Brisbane Line.

MacArthur saw this as the psychosis of defeat. Yet these were a brave and hardy people, who needed only to be reminded of their own strength. He scrapped the Brisbane Line.

"We shall make the fight for Australia in New Guinea," he told them. And for the first time since the Japanese had reached the Solomon Sea, the people of Australia began to feel secure.

The Japanese were at the peak of their power. Never had any invading forces seized control of so vast an area of land and sea, with so many natural resources, in so short time. MacArthur had neither a definite theater nor even general instructions. And he had no army.

Such American troops as had arrived were artillery, engineers, and a few Air Force units, with 250 worn-out or outmoded planes. Although three splendid Australian divisions were en route home from Egypt, until they arrived he would have only Australian militia. He lacked even one single infantry division. He had no tanks, no landing craft, and very few long-range bombers. Nevertheless, he began making plans to take the offensive.

He was not without some opposition, however. Although Admiral Ernest J. King, Chief of Naval Operations and Commander-in-Chief of the Navy, believed, like MacArthur, that the war in the Pacific was too important to be delayed, he insisted that the Navy should run it.

Despite the fact that the Army had to supply all of the logistical support except water transportation, and some 90 per cent of the men, King insisted that all joint operations should be under navy command—that army troops should assume the same relatively subordinate status as Marines. MacArthur's vast experience in war and his knowledge of the Japanese were to be ignored.

The President, however, knew MacArthur's great ability, and he was mindful of the Australian insistence that Mac-Arthur command in the Southwest Pacific. He drew an arbitrary line. The vast Central Pacific area would be under Admiral Chester W. Nimitz. In the Southwest Pacific, Mac-Arthur would be supreme. In between them, a South Pacific area command would operate in the Solomons.

Under MacArthur's prodding, a few troops and supplies began to flow toward Australia—two infantry divisions and auxiliary troops. But the best equipment, and the most modern tanks, all went to Europe.

On July 29 he received an able lieutenant in Major General George C. Kenney, who was to command his air force. Immediately mutual confidence was born. In a few days Kenney had so revitalized the scattered and dispirited air force personnel that on August 7, the day the Marines landed on Guadalcanal, he was able to strike the Japanese air base at Vunnakanau with eighteen B-17's, the first real Allied air strike of the Pacific war.

Rabaul, on the northeast tip of New Britain, was the key to the whole invasion area. The Japanese had seized it in January but had not yet built it up defensively. MacArthur proposed to use all of the American resources in the area, combined under one head, to surprise and capture Rabaul. The Japanese would be blocked and their bases in the Solomons would be isolated.

MacArthur had two homely precepts: "All there is to know is when and where to fight" and "always hit 'em where they ain't." This operation fitted both. It was the time and place to fight. Rabaul was lightly defended and thus vulnerable to MacArthur's second precept.

Admiral King thought the plan too risky. He preferred the slower policy of capturing each island separately—a series of bloody Guadalcanals. General Marshall supported him. So Rabaul remained in Japanese hands, and became a thorn in MacArthur's side.

In New Guinea, MacArthur moved quickly to checkmate two Japanese advances toward Port Moresby. He established a forward headquarters there. To reach it, the Japanese sent one force to take Milne Bay, at the tip of New Guinea, and another across the Owen Stanley Mountains, from strong bases at Buna and Gona, on the east coast.

MacArthur studied the probabilities. Kokoda Pass, high in the mountains, imposed cruel obstacles. He was confident that the Australian militia could hold it.

To Milne Bay, where American Engineers were building landing strips, he sent two militia brigades and a few Australian Regulars.

Before dawn on August 26 the Japanese began landing in force. A surprise awaited them. Air strikes disrupted the landing, and the Australians and the Engineers opened a withering fire from the jungle. When the fighting was over, a few of the Japanese were fleeing. The rest were dead.

Miles from its objective, the Japanese mountain column met defeat. Broken, it began the weary march back to Buna. Port Moresby was secure.

MacArthur ordered forward the 32nd Division, which had

been training in Australia. Its objective was Buna. By all usual standards, he had barely enough force to defend Australia; yet he was assuming the offensive. At Buna the inexperienced men of the 32nd found themselves mired down in an almost impenetrable jungle, facing tough, battle-wise Japanese, who were expertly fortified on dry ground.

In August a splendid ground force commander had joined MacArthur—Lieutenant General Robert L. Eichelberger. "I am putting you in command at Buna," MacArthur told him. "I want you to take Buna . . . or not come back alive!"

Eichelberger took Buna, *and returned alive.* Then Gona fell to the Allied arms, and the first American Army victory in the Pacific was announced to a waiting world. MacArthur had set his foot on the road back.

At Port Moresby, General Kenney established repair shops and maintenance facilities. By shortening the distance to the enemy's bases, he could make twice the strikes with the same number of planes . . . and he could supply the infantry at Buna. Without Kenney's leadership, and the labors of his 5th Air Force, MacArthur's supply problems would have been insurmountable.

MacArthur stimulated the morale of the newly created 5th Air Force by delegating to Kenney authority to award decorations for bravery or initiative immediately following the event. "Later" might be too late.

When rear-echelon MP's harassed battle-weary pilots and crews, on leave in Australia, MacArthur ordered the MP's to desist. The overworked men of the 5th Air Force were carrying America's hopes on the wings of their battered planes. Weird dress and escape-valve antics could be overlooked in the men who were doing the fighting . . . the men who were killing Japanese and seeing their comrades die.

He saw to it that Kenney had complete freedom of action, and that his own staff stayed "off of Kenney's back." No finer working relationship had ever been developed in war.

"If Douglas MacArthur decides that he has confidence in you," Kenney would say later, "he goes all the way."

Sheer necessity had made Buna a frontal operation; but the prompt efficiency with which Kenney's planes had supplied the jungle-bound 32nd Division had opened MacArthur's eyes to new possibilities. Billy Mitchell had expounded the theory of air power; now George Kenney had demonstrated its practical application. In MacArthur's hands, it would become a precision tool.

Air power enabled him to develop the "bypass," his economical technique of working past strongly held bases—such as Truk—and capturing weakly held ones far in their rear. Cut off from supplies, the Japanese would "wither on the vine," by the principle of surprise adapted to the air age.

There would be heavy fighting—desperate fighting. But lives would not be wasted. And if the ensuing months spelled toil and misery to the Americans and Australians as they slogged their way up the north coast of New Guinea, they spelled death and defeat to the Japanese.

In the Central Pacific, the Navy had broken the back of Japan's naval power at the Battle of Midway. Now it was engaged in "island hopping" its way toward Japan . . . delivering costly frontal assaults against such strongholds as Tarawa and Kwajalein.

Although MacArthur was hampered for lack of adequate naval support, the Navy kept on slugging its bloody way from one island to another . . . islands which he believed should be passed by. To his sorrow, soldiers and marines paid the price.

In Congress, Senator Chandler of Kentucky led a move to place MacArthur in supreme command of all Allied operations in the Pacific, and to adopt his strategy of approaching Japan via the Philippines. Manila Bay and northern Luzon would provide far better bases than any of the Pacific islands, he pointed out, and, with American bombers and submarines based in the Philippines, the Japanese would be cut off from supplies of rubber, tin, and oil, upon which their war industry depended.

King, backed by Marshall, disagreed. Iwo Jima and Okinawa would be the cost.

When the new rank of General of the Army was created, MacArthur was at first ignored. Only Marshall, Eisenhower, and Arnold were considered for the super grade. An angry storm righted matters, and he too was accorded the new honor.

Successes did nothing to add to MacArthur's popularity in Washington. His friends still did him incalculable harm by continuing to use his name as a possible presidential candidate. Earlier he had stated emphatically that, "I have no political ambitions whatsoever. I started as a soldier and I shall finish as one." But the well-meaning activities of his admirers continued to sound their own alarm.

A rumor spread that he was to be relieved from his command and brought home . . . to be "shelved" in a planning assignment. Then a fresh revulsion against the Japanese swept the country. To avoid public insistence upon more emphasis on the war in the Pacific, the news had been suppressed for days. Now it was out. Two of the Doolittle raiders, whose plane had been shot down over Tokyo, had been brutally abused. Finally they had been beheaded. America was enraged.

It was not the time to risk dumping a popular General who was busy killing Japanese.

11.

THE PRESIDENT DECIDES

✂ MacArthur's immediate problem was the elimination of the strong enemy bases at Lae, Salamaua, and Finschhafen, across Vitiaz Straight from New Britain. Since he needed them to advance Kenney's fighter bases, they could not be bypassed. But he wanted no more Bunas.

In February an old friend had joined him—Lieutenant General Walter Krueger, whose slowly arriving Sixth Army would form the backbone of the advance up the New Guinea coast and on to the Philippines. Naval support had grown. Rear Admiral Daniel E. Barbey had assembled enough landing craft to support a coastal operation. The 503rd Parachute Regiment had reached New Guinea.

MacArthur used the landing craft to put the 9th Australian

Division—the tough, competent "Rats of Tobruk"—ashore at Hopoi Bay, east of Lae.

Next morning more than three hundred planes took off from New Guinea bases. Their objective was the Japanese airdrome at Nadzab, twenty miles northwest of Lae. In the lead were B-25's, each mounting eight .50-caliber machine guns. Squadrons of C-47 transports carried the 503rd and a battery of Australian artillery. A B-17 carried an important passenger—Douglas MacArthur. He wanted to determine for himself the practicability of this new technique.

Precisely on schedule, the 503rd and the Aussie artillery made the Allies' first large-scale air drop against an enemy. The airdrome was seized and quickly became an American fighter base.

Several days were required to exterminate the last of the Lae garrison but, caught between the paratroopers and the "Rats of Tobruk," they died. In a few more days Salamaua and Finschhafen fell and the entire Huon Peninsula was cleared of the enemy.

On January 2, 1944, Saidor, some ninety miles northwest of Lae, fell to a surprise assault and became MacArthur's base of operations. Diaries taken from dead Japanese revealed the dismay that MacArthur's swift advance was creating, the heavy losses suffered by the enemy, and the destruction of their supplies by Kenney's bombers.

In December Vice Admiral Thomas C. Kinkaid's Seventh Fleet had come under MacArthur's command. At last he had complete control over a fleet capable of supporting a contested landing.

In July he was given strategical control over Admiral William F. Halsey's Third Fleet, which was operating in the

Solomons. But it was a less workable arrangement. Halsey commanded the South Pacific area, and he reported also to Admiral Nimitz, who controlled his ships, troops, and supplies.

Nevertheless, it was a splendid team. The austere Mac-Arthur and the breezy Halsey formed an immediate liking for each other. Each was a practical realist and an instinctive fighter.

More than a quarter million Japanese still stood between MacArthur and the recapture of the Philippines. But he was determined that as many as possible would be bypassed and left to die of starvation.

Rabaul, now heavily fortified, menaced MacArthur's advance. From it enemy bombers could strike his flank once he had passed beyond the Vitiaz Strait into the Bismarck Sea.

MacArthur prepared to isolate Rabaul. His first move was to seize Manus, in the Admiralty Islands. In the meantime, at the new Saidor base, plans were pushed to reduce Madang, Hansa Bay, and Wewak.

Although MacArthur's G-2 reported some four thousand Japanese on Manus, Kenney's pilots found that Los Negros, a neighboring island, was lightly held. MacArthur acted swiftly. On February 29 several destroyers, with a squadron of the 5th Cavalry aboard, entered Los Negros harbor. After a short preliminary bombardment, the troops landed. Mac-Arthur was with them.

Later a young cavalryman, who had gone forward with MacArthur, told a buddy about it.

"You mean General Chase, don't you?" the buddy insisted.

"No, dammit, I mean General MacArthur!" the first trooper

blazed. "He was right there with us. He ain't afraid of nothin'."

Reinforcements arrived, and in a few days Manus itself was taken. Quickly and at small cost, the Admiralties were in American hands. Their sudden capture had isolated Rabaul, and doomed the bypassed Japanese on New Britain and in the Solomons to slow starvation. And it opened to Mac-Arthur his greatest opportunity to "hit 'em where they ain't."

Some five hundred miles west of Saidor was Hollandia, the Japanese base of supplies. A surprise move from Manus to Hollandia would bypass heavily defended areas and secure a splendid base only eight hundred miles from the Philippines. Hollandia would be a rich prize.

On April 21 a vast fleet of three hundred ships, which had assembled secretly at Manus, sailed northwest. Japanese planes reported the startling armada, but mystery shrouded its destination. Their Intelligence predicted a probable landing "between Madang and Hansa." The Wewak area was next in probability. Hollandia was considered only as a "possibility." No one, the Japanese believed, would attempt so daring a move.

During the night the ships changed course, and the different task units bore toward their respective objectives.

When dawn revealed no threat to Madang, Hansa Bay, or Wewak, the Japanese were puzzled. Then the storm broke, far beyond their reach.

The surprise was so complete that there were few casualties. Most of the Japanese fled into the jungle, leaving arms, equipment, even uneaten breakfasts behind. Vast quantities of supplies were captured including—to the troops' huge delight—large caches of Japanese beer. It was a cheaply bought major victory.

Behind them, the Japanese Eighteenth Army was trapped. It would suffer the fate of its bypassed brethren in the Solomons.

Immediately Hollandia became a great supply base and staging area for the move toward the Philippines. Its growth was so rapid that it gave rise to the legend of the "million-dollar mansion" which "MacArthur had built on Lake Sentani for his family." Actually, the building was a "neat-looking structure of rough timber," which housed his entire head-quarters. MacArthur and his family, whom he had brought forward from Brisbane, occupied only two rooms.

In Washington the Navy had pressed upon the President a plan to bypass the Philippines, and to attempt to capture the key Japanese-fortified island of Formosa, the heart of the enemy defenses in the China Seas. MacArthur protested both the costly aspects of so dangerous an attempt and the de-liberate betrayal of the Filipinos.

In June, 1944, MacArthur was ordered to attend a confer-ence with the President at Pearl Harbor. But he was refused any explanation as to the purpose of the meeting. When he arrived, he found that the Navy was prepared, with maps, charts, and prepared arguments, to "sell" their Formosa plan.

Admiral Leahy, the President's Chief of Staff and an old friend, greeted MacArthur warmly. Leahy had first known him as "a handsome young officer in San Francisco, back in 1905" and he had "always entertained an extremely high opinion of his ability." Leahy was not in sympathy with the plans of his navy colleagues.

It was the first time that they had met in many years.

Leahy was surprised that "unlike the battle-worn Generals Chennault and Stilwell . . . MacArthur showed no strain other than looking a little tired."

Leahy watched MacArthur and the President greet each other with obvious pleasure. The closeness of their former relationship has seldom been fully understood. When he was Chief of Staff, MacArthur had been puzzled when the President discussed matters with him which were foreign to his duties. Finally he had asked the reason. Roosevelt laughed.

"Douglas," he had replied, "these are controversial matters. I have not sought your opinions but your reactions. To me, you symbolize the conscience of the American people."

After dinner the President opened the conference. He called upon Admiral Nimitz to present the Navy's plan to approach Japan via Formosa.

Skillfully, Nimitz built up the Navy's case. It sounded plausible. Roosevelt was impressed. His eyes brightened at the promise to "carry the war to the enemy."

In MacArthur's opinion, the Navy had always fought well but not necessarily wisely. In its natural element, combat at sea, it had performed epic deeds of valor; but whenever it essayed the Army's role, the results had been costly. In his area, the Southwest Pacific, more than a thousand miles of enemy territory, all taken at small loss, more than two hundred thousand bypassed Japanese and thousands of enemy dead testified that his limited forces had fought both wisely and well. It angered MacArthur that pressures were being brought to bear to advance the costlier means of accomplishing the same ends.

Even when he learned that most of his forces were to be

taken away, and that he was to be left to "clean out" the lower Philippines and Dutch East Indies, MacArthur would not permit indignation to rob him of his major weapon—eloquence.

At last MacArthur was called upon to present the case for an approach to Japan via the Philippines. He had no maps, no rehearsed arguments. He had only a conviction born of his insight, and an unswerving sense of duty to the Filipino people, who looked to him for liberation.

He spoke of the high esteem in which he held Admiral Nimitz and his associates, and of his admiration for their victories at sea; but he stated immediately that he rejected their policy of making frontal assaults against such strongly held islands as Saipan, Iwo Jima, and Okinawa. He warned that the losses would be far too heavy for any benefit to be gained. They were not, in his opinion, essential to the enemy's defeat.

As for any actual value that Formosa might have, he pointed out that its lack of natural resources and its hostile population would largely nullify its usefulness as a base from which to attack Japan. He was critical of the orginal failure to save the Philippines—of the lack of the initiative that later characterized the Navy's success in supplying the Russians, through far more dangerous waters. Deliberately to sacrifice the Philippines a second time, he warned, would neither be forgotten nor condoned.

There were two reasons, he explained, why the Philippines must be reoccupied. Militarily their possession would cut off the flow of raw materials to Japan, thus paralyzing her war industries. Psychologically a failure to drive out the

Japanese, and to liberate both the native Filipinos and the thousands of American prisoners, would never be understandable to the Oriental mind. America's honor must be redeemed.

Patiently the President heard him out. Obviously he was moved, but he still seemed to be in doubt.

"But to take Luzon would entail even heavier losses," he demurred. "It seems to me, Douglas, that it would be much cheaper to bypass the Philippines."

"No, Mr. President," MacArthur replied. "My losses would be no heavier than they have been in the past. The day of the frontal attack is over. Only inexperienced or mediocre commanders still use it. Your good commanders do not turn in heavy losses."

The President deferred his decision until the next day. Ostensibly he wanted time to consider the two points of view.

As MacArthur was leaving, Admiral Leahy leaned toward him and whispered, "I'll go along with you, Douglas."

Later that evening MacArthur spent a little time with the President alone. It was like earlier days in the White House. He spoke his mind in warning Roosevelt of the potential political consequences of bypassing the Philippines.

"If you leave our people to die, Mr. President," he warned, "public opinion will condemn you. And it will be justified!"

Next morning, the Commander-in-Chief accepted MacArthur's recommendations. The Philippine plan was approved. Admiral Nimitz would continue to move directly toward Japan, but there would be no Formosa adventure.

One serious fault had not been remedied. Although it

would remain under his strategic direction, Halsey's Third Fleet would still not be under MacArthur's direct command. It would support him, but it would not "obey" him. It was a loose arrangement that would come frighteningly near to turning victory into disaster.

12.

"RALLY TO ME!"

✗ Back at Hollandia, MacArthur pushed plans to land on Mindanao, but not before December 20, 1944. Morotai, three hundred miles south of Mindanao, was taken to use as an air base.

On nearby Halmahera 250 Japanese were destroyed or routed, and a garrison of twenty thousand Japanese was bypassed. With Morotai seized and Halmahera eliminated, fifteen hundred miles of neutralized territory, and several hundred thousand helpless Japanese, lay behind MacArthur. Ahead lay the Philippines.

Carrier-borne planes from Halsey's Third Fleet supported the Morotai landing by bombing airfields on Mindanao. A navy pilot, who had been shot down over Leyte and rescued by Filipino guerrillas, reported that Leyte was lightly held. Although the report was considerably in error, it spurred fast action.

Immediately Halsey recommended that landings be made on Leyte rather than on Mindanao; and, in view of the light opposition to be expected, he recommended that the date be advanced. Nimitz agreed, and expressed to Admiral King his willingness to cooperate with MacArthur.

The Joint Chiefs of Staff were in Quebec, with Roosevelt and Churchill. Favoring the idea, they asked MacArthur for his opinion. His reply reached them quickly.

"I am prepared to move immediately upon Leyte," he radioed, "with target date of October 20. . . ."

The new date set was, as MacArthur had suggested, October 20. When the time arrived, all things were ready except one—there was still no unity of command. In other theaters, where nationalities as well as rival services were involved, all major commands were unified.

"Of all the faulty decisions of the war," MacArthur said later, "the most unexplainable one was the failure to unify the command in the Pacific. The failure . . . cannot be defended in logic, in theory, or even common sense. Other motives must be ascribed."

In the intricate operations which lay ahead, any emergency which involved both services could be met only after Nimitz had been consulted. At Leyte the delay would be costly.

The Japanese had not been asleep. Obviously a landing in the Philippines was next on MacArthur's agenda. They prepared for it.

General Tomoyuki Yamashita, the "Tiger of Malaya," had

been brought from Manchuria to "...stop MacArthur. He was a dangerous foe."

Since the loss of the Philippines would be disastrous, the Japanese threw every resource into the effort to hold them—troops from other areas, aircraft from their dwindling reserves, even the great 64,000-ton battleships *Yamato* and *Musachi*. As General Shuichi Miyazake summed it up:

> ...holding the Philippines was the one essential... with the loss of these islands, Japanese communications with the southern region would be severely threatened. The loss would affect civilian morale in Japan. The islands were essential as a strategic base for the enemy advance on Japan. After their recapture, the advantage would be two to one in favor of the Americans.

The Japanese General Staff would have welcomed the Navy's plan to bypass these vital islands and attack Japan's close-in defenses.

The Japanese Navy was still a formidable force. Although widely dispersed, powerful task forces could rendezvous quickly. Two such forces, approaching through Surigao Strait south of Leyte, and San Bernardino Strait to its north, could converge on the landing areas at Leyte like twin besoms of destruction. If a third task force, moving down the east coast of Luzon, could lure the covering forces north to meet it, MacArthur's huge amphibious force would be in grave danger.

Strong naval forces would have to block the approaches to Leyte Gulf, where the invaders would land. Kinkaid, who answered directly to MacArthur, disposed his units to cover the approaches through Surigao Strait. Halsey, operating independently, was depended upon to patrol San Bernardino Strait as well as to provide air cover. Kenney's bases were still too distant for his planes to cover the landing. For this first time, therefore, MacArthur had violated his own principle of never moving beyond range of air protection. Without a unified command, great risks were involved.

Although severe storms and heavy seas had made preliminary tasks difficult, the sun of October 20 rose over an untroubled sea. At dawn, on board the cruiser *Nashville*, MacArthur had awakened to the distant rumble of the naval bombardment of enemy shore defenses.

After breakfast he walked out on the flag bridge. All about him, as far as the eye could see, rode the greatest armada that the Pacific had ever seen. In March, 1942—thirty-one months ago—he had left the Philippines a fugitive, with only four PT boats and a small staff. Now he was returning with a fleet of more than 650 ships—some of them the world's mightiest —and a force of 150,000 men.

Asked by General Courtney Whitney, the director of the far-flung guerrilla forces in the Philippines, if so mighty a command did not give him a great sense of power, he replied, "No, Court, it doesn't. I cannot escape the thought of the fine American boys who are going to die on those beaches."

Initially the landing forces met relatively light resistance. Surprise had thrown the Japanese off balance. As they recovered, they fought savagely; but they were forced back to the hills, where General Makina's 16th Division—notorious for its brutalities on Bataan—was building formidable defenses.

Within ten days five airfields were in American hands. Since the weather was usually fair at this season, MacArthur had planned to move Kenney's fighters and bombers into them immediately to relieve himself of the risk of depending upon air support which he did not command. This year unseasonable rains turned the fields into useless bogs. He was forced to depend upon Halsey.

Near Palo, a few miles south of Tacloban, MacArthur waded ashore from a landing barge which had followed the third assault wave. With him were President Sergio Osmeña, who had succeeded Quezon, Krueger, Kenney, Whitney, Romulo, and a few others. On the beach he paused for a moment as though to grasp the full reality of the scene. After two years and seven months of dedicated labors, he was back on Philippine soil. He had returned.

The third wave was just working its way through burning palms, and men were ducking instinctively at the sharp *blat* of Japanese bullets, when MacArthur strode forward to get a better view of the situation. A crouching GI stared at him in amazement.

"Look!" he called to his squad leader. "There's General MacArthur!"

Intent on watching for the signal to advance, the sergeant didn't even look around. "Yeah!" he scoffed. "And I suppose that he's got Eleanor Roosevelt with him!"

Down the beach a mobile broadcasting unit had been set up. The "Voice of Freedom" was returning to the air on Philippine soil.

Romulo had prepared a proclamation for delivery by MacArthur—a message which would stir the hearts of the deeply religious Filipinos. It contained eloquent words—inspiring words.

"To the people of the Philippines," he began, emotionally.

"This is the Voice of Freedom, General MacArthur speaking. I have returned. By the grace of Almighty God, our forces stand again on Philippine soil... soil consecrated in the blood of our two peoples. We have come, dedicated and committed, to the task of restoring the liberties... of your people.

"At my side is your President, Sergio Osmeña, worthy successor of that patriot Manuel Quezon... the seat of your government is now therefore re-established on Philippine soil.

"Rally to me! Let the indomitable spirit of Bataan and Corregidor lead on. As the battle lines roll forward... rise and strike! For your homes and hearths, strike! In the name of your sacred dead, strike! Let no heart be faint! Let every arm be steeled! The guidance of divine God points the way! Follow in His name to the Holy Grail of righteous victory!"

The Philippine people were electrified. MacArthur had returned! From village to village, the word spread with the speed of sound. Liberation was near at hand.

The proclamation was intended for Filipino ears only. They heard it with rejoicing... and they struck. Unfortunately it was released for publication in the United States. MacArthur critics sneered at his emotionalism, and took issue with his references to the Almighty.

"In war," he had previously said, "when a commander... fails to understand the dependence of arms on Divine guidance, he no longer deserves victory."

On October 23, three days later, MacArthur and Osmeña entered Tacloban, the capital of the province. In a solemn ceremony the flags of the United States and the Philippines were raised. Then, before the assembled people, MacArthur restored to President Osmeña all of his constitutional powers within the area.

The next night a fast Japanese force entered Surigao Strait to surprise the few ships thought to be stationed there and to clear a path for a heavier force which was following. The surprise failed.

Strong elements of the Seventh Fleet, under Rear Admiral Jesse B. Oldendorf, lashed out in the darkness with destructive destroyer and PT boat attacks. Battleships took heavy toll of the confused Japanese. By dawn the enemy had lost two battleships and three destroyers. A mortally damaged heavy cruiser sank while attempting to escape.

The second Japanese force, seeing the destruction to the leading group, turned to withdraw; but it lost a light cruiser and two destroyers to American air attacks. Thanks to the vigilance of the Seventh Fleet, two Japanese task forces had been defeated. It was the last naval battle in which great battleships engaged with each other with decisive effect.

Farther north a far more powerful Japanese force, whose battle line included the *Musachi* and the *Yamato*, was moving through San Bernardino Strait. Its commander, Admiral Takeo Kurita, was daring and resourceful.

A fourth force, under Admiral Ozawa, moved down the east coast of Luzon to attract Halsey's attention. In San Bernardino Strait, Kurita was attacked repeatedly by Halsey's planes. The *Musachi* was sunk and several cruisers and destroyers damaged. These attacks caused Kurita to turn back to assess his damage, but he did not abandon his mission.

Eager to speed north to intercept Ozawa, Halsey seized upon overly optimistic reports that Kurita had retired. It was what he wanted to hear. Immediately he started north. Earlier he had organized his battleships into a task force—Task Force 34—to attack Kurita. Believing Kurita already defeated, he took it with him.

Under cover of darkness Kurita returned. Dawn found him nearing the lightly defended transports and cargo vessels upon which the success of the invasion depended.

Before dawn premonition had prompted Kinkaid to ask Halsey, "Is TF 34 guarding San Bernardino Strait?" Three hours later the terrible answer came: "TF 34 is with carrier group."

Kinkaid's primary responsibility was the protection of the south approaches to the anchorages of Leyte. His battleships and cruisers were disposed for that task. At the anchorages he had nothing but Rear Admiral Thomas L. Sprague's small escort carriers and a few destroyers with which to meet Kurita's threat. They did so gallantly.

At 6:37 A.M. the escort carrier *Fanshaw Bay* discovered the enemy. At 6:48 *Yamato's* eighteen-inch guns opened.

For almost two and one-half hours Kurita pressed his advantage. Victory was almost within his grasp. Then fate intervened. Learning the fate of the forces in Surigao Strait, and uncertain of Halsey's position, he broke off the attack and retired. Had he pressed on, he could have destroyed the remaining combat ships and wreaked irreparable havoc among the helpless vessels upon which MacArthur depended.

Halsey was too far to the north to protect the troops on Leyte, and the anchorages, with naval air cover. Since Mac-Arthur could not order him back, he radioed to Nimitz—at Pearl Harbor, five thousand miles away—requesting that it be done. Nimitz was unable to contact Halsey.

Despite the near disaster, and the casualties which his troops had suffered without the promised naval air support, MacArthur never blamed Halsey. The danger had passed. Besides, war was not only full of uncertainties and confusion —it was, as Sherman said, "hell."

As Krueger's Sixth Army troops battered at the skillfully built "Yamashita Line," the fighting became fiercer and more bloody. In desperation the Japanese had rushed seasoned troops from China and Manchuria to make Leyte MacArthur's Waterloo. They failed. Despite the costly delay, MacArthur managed to hold the initiative by applying constant but slow pressure on the enemy.

"I can take Leyte in two more weeks," he told correspondents who questioned his apparent slowness, "but I won't. I have too great a responsibility to the mothers and wives in America. I will not take by sacrifice what I can achieve by strategy. I have seen too many lives wasted unnecessarily in battle."

Despite his brilliant victories and his care in preserving men's lives, MacArthur's relations with the press had not been good. Correspondents complained that his press releases were not fully informative, and that he did not play up senior subordinates in the news.

In the Southwest Pacific life hung on a thin shoestring. He was adamant in maintaining complete secrecy, and the doings of his higher commanders could reveal intended moves to enemy intelligence analysts. As a result the Japanese were seldom able to fathom his intentions, and his losses were correspondingly light. Secrecy paid off, but it won him the enmity of a few members of the press. He paid no heed.

There were also other problems. In other areas combat

troops were afforded opportunities for rest and recreation. MacArthur was assigned no ships to transport his battle-weary men to rest areas. Their principal recreation was an occasional motion picture or USO troupe, presented in the rain.

It was unfortunate that his men seldom saw him. In Europe good motor roads enabled even senior commanders to become well acquainted with their men. In the Southwest Pacific there were no roads. Except at air strips and on landing beaches, MacArthur was seldom seen. As a result he was a remote figure, unknown and misunderstood. His old Rainbow men, to whom he was still their "hell to breakfast Brigadier," would have been puzzled; but they had been able to know and understand him. He had been just as careful of these men's lives, and as active in their behalf, as he had been of his Rainbow men. It was both his misfortune and theirs that they had no way of knowing it.

Then, on December 28 MacArthur delivered the *coup de grâce* to the Japanese defenders of Leyte. Ormoc, on the west coast, was Yamashita's base. MacArthur sent the 77th Division to eliminate it. By a surprise amphibious landing on the beaches south of the town, the 77th seized Ormoc and severed Yamashita's communications. Turning east, they struck the rear of the "Yamashita Line" and split the defenders into two confused masses. Caught between the Sixth Army in their front, and an enemy of unknown strength in their rear, the Japanese sought refuge on higher ground.

Two weeks of savage fighting followed, but on December 26 MacArthur could announce that organized resistance had ceased. But he indulged himself in no false sense of elation. Luzon still lay ahead.

On December 18 during the heaviest of the fighting, he had been promoted to the newly created grade of "General of the Army." He would wear five stars now, to denote his rank, but they would not lighten his load. Some of his hardest work remained to be done. Then greater challenges would loom.

13.

DEFENDER—LIBERATOR

✗   Luzon presented a difficult problem. Despite his losses on Leyte, Yamashita's forces were still numerically greater than MacArthur's, even though the latter now had two field armies—Krueger's Sixth and Eichelberger's Eighth—under his command.

MacArthur's plan for this last phase of his brilliant Pacific campaigns was a model of simplicity.

"With my Eighth Army off the southern coast of Luzon," he told the Joint Chiefs of Staff, "I will threaten landings at southern ports and draw the bulk of the Japanese into the south. This done, I will land the Sixth Army on the exposed northern shore, thus cutting off the enemy's supplies from Japan. This will draw the enemy back to the north, leaving the Eighth Army to land against only weak opposition. Both forces will then close like a vise on the enemy and destroy him."

Yamashita's forces—estimated at 235,000 men—were organized for a desperate resistance. High in Luzon's mountainous terrain, their defensive positions were strongly fortified. Weapons, ammunition, and huge stocks of food had been stored in preparation for a protracted siege. At key points, tanks—immobilized by lack of gasoline—were buried in the ground to serve as pillboxes. They provided interlocking bands of machine-gun and tank cannon fire.

Stung by his defeat on Leyte, Yamashita was coldly determined that MacArthur would be made to pay. The suicidal fanaticism of his soldiers reflected his determination.

On the 5th the cruiser *Boise,* flying MacArthur's five-star flag, moved through the deep blue waters off the west coast of Luzon. MacArthur paced the bridge leisurely, as though on a pleasure cruise. Suddenly a torpedo streaked across the water toward the *Boise.* Full speed and a quick change of course saved the ship. Depth bombs from a nearby destroyer brought a midget submarine to the surface, only to be rammed and sunk by the charging destroyer.

Next morning he was again on the bridge when the cruiser's loud-speaker crackled a warning. Enemy planes were attacking. One dropped a bomb perilously close. Another dived, then veered off and disappeared as a storm of antiaircraft fire broke from the *Boise's* guns. A third was hit and crashed into the sea close by.

Again MacArthur watched imperturbably. A sailor at a nearby gun stared in wonder. "That guy's all right," he told his mate. "He stands out here like the rest of us and takes it."

As the far-flung convoy passed them, MacArthur could see familiar landmarks—Mariveles, Bataan, Corregidor, Manila. In a sense he was returning home.

At dawn on the 9th they arrived off Lingayen Gulf and stood in toward shore. By nine-thirty the first assault waves approached the beaches.

Hundreds of landing craft churned shoreward with their tense, battle-ready cargoes. Tanks, bulldozers, trucks, ammunition, and artillery were poured ashore behind the infantry. Bedlam prevailed, but near-faultless planning reduced confusion to the minimum.

As MacArthur had predicted, the threat from Mindoro had drawn Yamashita south. Now he hurried north again; but, harassed by guerrillas and by Kenney's planes, his tired columns became entangled in traffic jams and lost vital time. The initiative remained in MacArthur's skilled hands.

By dark sixty-eight thousand troops were ashore. They were deployed on a seventeen-mile arc with a depth of four miles. Dirty and tired, they dug in and got what rest they could through the uncertain night. MacArthur himself was everywhere. His Philippine Marshal cap became a familiar sight to the troops. His presence roused the Filipino people to excited confidence. They would soon be free.

Yamashita hurried his troops into their formidable positions in time to check most of the American advance. MacArthur was unconcerned. He was safely established on Luzon. In the mountainous area which he had chosen to defend, Yamashita could be destroyed at leisure.

Weeks of bloody fighting lay ahead, but MacArthur intended no massed assaults. He was determined that the cost to his men would be as small as good planning could make it. For the time being he was more intent on pushing Krueger's right steadily forward toward Manila, to link up with Eichelberger's advance from the south. He had a mission of mercy to perform. Aware of the pitiable plight of the American and Allied prisoners in Japanese hands, he was determined to save them.

By the 30th he was within reach of the prison near Cabanatuan. He sent 134 men from the 6th Ranger Battalion, guided by tough Filipino guerrillas, to seize it. Darkness had fallen when, after a daring raid through enemy-held country, they surprised and killed the guards. More than five hundred American and Allied soldiers were saved.

The sick and emaciated men were helped back through the enemy lines to the liberated town of Guimba. There, early next morning, MacArthur met them. Their condition sharpened his resolve to reach the remaining prisons quickly.

Many of these men were survivors of Bataan and Corregidor. Some of them had cursed him for "deserting" them. But their bitterness disappeared as they realized that had MacArthur not gone he could not have returned, and his return had saved their lives. They were filled with pride as he told them how their stubborn defense had saved Australia, and prepared the way for Japan's sure destruction.

On the following day—February 1—he sent the 1st Cavalry Division on a headlong dash through a hundred miles of enemy-held country to rescue the thirty-five hundred men and children held in Santo Tomás University, in Manila. At dark on the 3rd the leading tank of the 44th Tank Battalion smashed through the prison gates.

The next day advanced units of the 37th Division, fighting their way into Manila, seized notorious Bilibid Prison and liberated a thousand more ragged, starving prisoners. At Los Banos, south of Manila and fifty miles inside the enemy lines, two thousand prisoners were held. Eichelberger sent a relief force to reach the prison. These troops, too, arrived in time.

On the 7th, four days after the daring cavalrymen had earned the distinction of being "first in Manila," MacArthur entered the city. Japanese shells were falling near Santo Tomâs as he stepped from a car at the prison gate. Inside old friends crowded around him to shake his hand. It was a scene of tears and of rejoicing. Sometimes, almost overcome with emotion, MacArthur walked through the whole prison, finding more old friends, encouraging the sick, seeing for himself the conditions under which they had managed to survive.

At Bilibid, in the military section of the prison, lines of men, ragged, emaciated, some in tears, stood at attention in forlorn pride. As he shook each man's hands, and heard their words of greeting, MacArthur swallowed hard.

"You're back," they said thankfully. "You made it."

All that he could reply was, "I'm long overdue. I'm long overdue."

In the streets, the people went wild. Shouting, "Veektory! Veektory!" they swarmed around the liberating troops and cheered them. Stripped of possessions themselves, they looted enemy-owned shops and stores to find presents to give to the soldiers.

For MacArthur, it was the end of a four-thousand-mile journey of fulfillment. A harsh journey, every step one of toil

and misery. Because he had made it, a nation had been reborn, and thousands of Americans and their Allied comrades
in arms would see their homes again.

Corregidor remained to be taken. Four thousand tons of
bombs dazed the Japanese defenders. Then paratroopers—
the battle-wise 503rd—dropped on "Topside," while a battalion of Indiana's 151st Infantry made a sudden landing on
the beach below. For eleven days the paratroops and the
Hoosiers flushed the bombardment-dazed enemy from tunnels and emplacements, killing as they progressed. When it
was over, 4,516 Japanese had been killed. The American dead
were 209. It was a typical MacArthur ratio.

With every member of his staff who had left Corregidor
with him, and symbolically in four PT boats, MacArthur returned to the island which he had left under such seemingly
hopeless conditions almost three years before.

What bitter memories crowded into his mind as he gazed
into the charnelhouse of Malinta Tunnel, his staff could only
surmise. But the hour of his greatest humiliation had long
since passed. Corregidor had been redeemed.

A familiar object caught his eye. "I see that the old flagpole still stands," he said. "Hoist the colors to its peak, and
let no enemy ever haul them down."

Manila had been destroyed. Famous public buildings were
mere shells, if they stood at all. Yet, to MacArthur's delight,
he found that the Malacañan Palace, which his father had
occupied as governor-general, forty-four years before, had
been left almost untouched.

On February 27 he strode through its crimson-brocaded
draperies to the state reception room, to complete at Manila

what he had begun at Tacloban—the restoration of the powers of the Commonwealth government. Five days later the last fanatical Japanese had been killed. Manila and its people were free. Immediately, with war still raging only a few miles away, the work of restoration was begun.

From all over the world congratulations poured into MacArthur's headquarters. He received the Thanks of Congress, followed by honors from Australia and other governments. Douglas Southall Freeman, distinguished historian and authority on Lee and his lieutenants, bestowed upon him a treasured accolade. Freeman said: "The true worth of a commander-in-chief is tested only in adversity . . . The immortal mantle of Lee and Jackson has fallen on your shoulders."

But there was still hard work ahead. It was not until June 28, after four more months of inch by inch fighting, that he could report that, "Except for isolated operations, this closes the major phases of the North Luzon Campaign, one of the most savage and bitterly fought in American history. . . ."

On April 12, 1945, President Roosevelt had died. President Truman now sent his congratulations to MacArthur, with the hope that "the powerful base we are now fashioning in the Philippines will play its full part in the final knock-out blow against Japan."

In the South China Sea one last major task remained. Borneo was still held by the Japanese. Immediately MacArthur set out to join General Blamey, whose Australians would do the work.

Landing in quick succession on the north, east, and south coasts of Borneo, the magnificent Aussies knocked the Japanese command off balance. The fighting lasted through three hard weeks. MacArthur remained until Blamey's forces were too firmly established to be driven back into the sea, no matter what the odds.

Again he had gone ashore with one of the assault waves, and led his small party into the Aussies' frontline. A photographer, poised to make a picture of the scene, was struck by a bullet fired by a Japanese hidden in a ditch, only a hundred feet from where MacArthur stood.

The danger seemed to exhilarate him. His staff members were not so fortunate. Brave enough to meet any actual demand, none of them found pleasure in deliberate exposure to enemy fire. Finally Kenney had had enough. Then, too, he had a way with MacArthur . . . also an appetite for ice cream. After reminding MacArthur that front-line combat was the infantry's affair, not the commander-in-chief's, he proposed that they return to the ship in time for dinner. He was hungry.

MacArthur took it good-naturedly.

"All right, George," he agreed. "I wouldn't have you miss your ice cream for anything."

Late in February, Secretary of the Navy Forrestal had visited him at Tarlac, close behind the battle line. During their conversation Forrestal revealed the navy opinion that the Chinese mainland should be invaded before attempting an invasion of Japan.

MacArthur was opposed to such a move. In his opinion, if Chiang were properly supplied, he could neutralize the Japanese forces on the China coast.

Navy planning, MacArthur learned, contemplated eighteen more months of war after Germany had been defeated. Forrestal asked his opinion.

"I predict," said MacArthur, "that the war will terminate this year." He pointed out that Japan had received devastating blows, and that both its navy and air force had been reduced to near impotence. Japan was approaching collapse, he insisted. The end would be sudden . . . possibly within six months. Yet he knew nothing of the atom bomb project. His predictions were based solely upon known factors.

Forrestal was amazed but not convinced. But he asked for and received MacArthur's permission to quote him in Washington. MacArthur was so firmly convinced of a sudden surrender that the Eighth Army staff was already preparing plans for a peaceful entry into Japan and the assumption of occupation duties.

MacArthur deplored the possible entry of Russia into the war against Japan. In 1942 he had urged it. Now the time of need had passed. Victory was at hand, and without Russian help.

MacArthur learned that Roosevelt, Churchill, and Stalin were secretly reshaping the postwar world. Although their agreements would undoubtedly affect all of Asia, his vast store of knowledge of Asiatic affairs was not sought.

At Tacloban, months before, he had expressed his fears to a group of correspondents. He was concerned lest the importance of Asia be discounted by postwar planners.

"The history of the world for the next thousand years will be written in the Pacific," he told them.

He foresaw the danger to world peace should Mao Tsetung supplant Chiang Kai-shek, and China cease to be a part of the free world.

Sensing the tendency of the liberals in Washington to accept Mao as an honest "agrarian reformer," who should have a dominant voice in the government of China, he was concerned lest they influence the Administration to abandon Chiang and permit China to go completely Communist.

In six short years his fears would be fully realized.

A few weeks later, at Yalta, concessions to their greed would place the Russians, and consequently the Red Chinese, on the highroad to dominant world power. It would be many more weeks before MacArthur would learn the ugly truth . . . that Russia had been persuaded to enter the war against Japan—when it was no longer needed.

Despite his conviction that victory was not far away, MacArthur proceeded with his planning for an invasion of Japan. He had been appalled at the terrible losses which the navy-managed attack on Okinawa had sustained. Now things would be different. The Joint Chiefs of Staff had taken one step toward unity of command in the Pacific—he had been appointed Commander-in-Chief, U. S. Army Forces in the Pacific. All naval elements passed to the command of Admiral Nimitz. At last the soldiers in the Central Pacific would have the same skilled concern for their lives that his men had had.

A few weeks later, when he was leaving the Philippines to receive the surrender of Japan, the Congress of the Philippines awarded him the most touching honors of all.

First, it conferred upon him honorary citizenship.

Second, it directed that "in reverent appreciation of General Douglas MacArthur, his name be carried in perpetuity on the company rolls of the units of the Philippine Army, and at parade roll calls, when his name is called, the senior non-commissioned officer shall answer 'Present in spirit.' "

Third, that "coins and postage stamps, to be determined by the President, having the likeness of General Douglas Mac-Arthur, shall bear the inscription:

" 'DEFENDER—LIBERATOR' "

14.

UNFURLING THE FLAG IN TOKYO

✗ In May the Germans surrendered. Allied efforts could be concentrated upon the defeat of Japan. Faced with this grim fact, the Japanese sought peace.

With victory over Japan merely a matter of time, people began to wonder about our postwar objectives. Would we deal generously with a mistaken people, and prepare them for a democratic future in a peaceful world? Or would we abandon them to a brutal enemy?

In America fierce controversies raged. Even within the government, the proponents of a westernized Japan, imbued with democratic ideals, clashed with those who insisted that Hirohito be hanged and his subjects turned over to the Russians.

MacArthur's attitude toward the Japanese was not one of revenge. Militarily he intended to conquer them; but he had no desire to crush them as a people. He would deal sternly with those who merited stern justice; but he hoped for a chance to gain the confidence of the people, and to lead them to a constructive place in an untroubled world.

Bombing raids had burned out vast areas of Japan's principal cities and made thousands homeless. Her war industries had dwindled to ineffectiveness. All hope had been lost. With the exception of fanatics who preferred death to surrender, the Japanese were ready for peace at almost any price. Yet most of the people were prepared to die rather than to forsake their Emperor. On this point peace negotiations failed.

Fortunately Secretary of War Stimson who, like MacArthur, understood the Japanese and their reverence for their hereditary ruler, managed to prevail upon President Truman to "guarantee the continuance of the Emperor's life and authority," provided that a democratic regime was established and maintained. It opened the way for an acceptable surrender.

It was not until July 29 that the Allied terms were promulgated—in the form of the Potsdam Proclamation to Japan. Before the Japanese could reconcile conflicting views within their government, atom bombs had blasted Hiroshima and Nagasaki. Hurriedly the Russians attacked the Japanese in Manchuria.

Appalled at the bombings, Hirohito himself took charge of the matter. He prepared a recording of a rescript of surrender, which was broadcast to the Japanese people.

On August 14, six days after the Russian entry, President Truman announced the Japanese acceptance of unconditional surrender terms. As MacArthur had expected, the war with Japan had been brought to an end without a costly invasion.

There was no over-all Allied commander to receive the surrender and to represent the Allied Powers as military governor of Japan.

Although both General Marshall and Admiral King were willing candidates, neither had ever exercised actual combat command; and none but a conqueror would be respected in Japan. Admiral Nimitz was the Navy's choice, but the President, too, had been appalled at the terrible losses in the Okinawa invasion. He chose the more widely experienced MacArthur as Supreme Commander for the Allied Powers.

MacArthur's first act was to direct the Japanese government to send emissaries to Manila who were "empowered to receive in the name of the Emperor . . . certain requirements for carrying into effect the terms of the surrender."

These emissaries reached Manila on August 19. MacArthur himself did not receive them. Instead, his Chief of Staff gave them his instructions.

They were instructed to prepare the excellent air base at Atsugi, ten miles from Yokohama, to receive American planes and to billet an airborne division; to prepare the New Grand Hotel, in Yokohama, for the use of MacArthur and his staff; and to provide transportation to that city. Demobilization of all Japanese forces was to begin immediately.

MacArthur was about to take the greatest chance of his career. Despite the misgivings of his staff, his faith in the Emperor's control over the Japanese people was such that he had decided to land in Japan only a few hours behind the 11th Airborne Division, which was to receive him. And the

Emperor's word was pledged by the terms of the surrender.

On August 30, before dawn, transport planes began taking off from Okinawa with the airborne troops. Eichelberger, whose Eighth Army had been selected to "occupy" Japan, accompanied the leading increments to arrange for MacArthur's arrival.

Eight hours after the first planes had departed, MacArthur's silvery C-54, the *Bataan*, lifted from the runway. During much of the flight MacArthur paced the aisle, deep in thought, or discussed plans for the governing of Japan with General Courtney Whitney, who was to be his Government Officer.

As the *Bataan* neared Japan tension seized many of the staff. Despite their faith in MacArthur's judgment, some were increasingly apprehensive. Stomachs tightened into painful knots. MacArthur was peacefully asleep.

About two o'clock the *Bataan* circled gracefully over the flat Kanto Plain and landed. As the ramp was let down the 11th Airborne's band commenced to play. Reporters and photographers—Allied, who had arrived with the troops, and Japanese—crowded forward.

MacArthur was addicted to smoking a corncob pipe. Like his cap, it had become a familiar part of him. Now, as he emerged from the plane, the men of the 11th Airborne saw that he was unarmed and that he was smoking his corncob pipe. It gave a touch of reassuring familiarity to a coldly hostile setting.

Eichelberger came forward to greet him, and MacArthur shook his hand warmly. It was the end of a long road which they had traveled together.

"Well, Bob," MacArthur said, "this is the pay-off."

He was amused when a brash Japanese photographer crowded ahead of an American cameraman. "Son," he advised the annoyed American, "you will have to make him capitulate."

A line of decrepit vehicles stood waiting—the best the Japanese could assemble. Headed by a ramshackle fire engine, the cavalcade started for Yokohama. Japanese troops lined the route. In the same token of respect to MacArthur which they always accorded the Emperor, they were posted with their backs to the road.

Next day MacArthur learned that General Wainwright and General Percival, the British commander at Singapore, had been liberated in Manchuria. He ordered them flown to Japan to attend the surrender.

MacArthur was at dinner when they arrived. He jumped up and met them at the door. He was shocked at their appearance. Wainwright's nickname "Skinny" had never suited him so well. He was a gaunt skeleton, as was Percival. Wainwright had accepted his ill treatment philosophically, but he harbored a deep sense of failure because he had been compelled to surrender Corregidor. He believed that he would never be restored to active duty.

MacArthur was shocked. To him, Wainwright's services had been of the highest order. No blame could be attached to him.

"Why, Jim," he protested, "you can have command of a corps with me any time you want it." Wainwright's relief was touching. He no longer felt disgraced.

The dawn of September 2, 1945, was one of symbolical foreboding for the defeated Japanese. Dull gray clouds hung low over Tokyo Bay, where a vast armada of Allied ships had been assembled.

At 8:55 the Japanese delegates—military and diplomatic—mounted the USS *Missouri*'s boarding ladder. On deck they faced a stern array of Allied officers, under whose cold eyes they fidgeted uncomfortably. Four minutes later MacArthur strode from Halsey's cabin.

In contrast to the correct attire of the eleven unhappy Japanese, MacArthur wore his customary open-necked shirt and khaki trousers. His manner expressed his contempt. He walked briskly to a bank of microphones which stood behind the table on which lay the surrender documents.

"We are gathered here," he began, "representatives of the major warring powers, to conclude a solemn agreement whereby peace may be restored. The issues, involving divergent ideals and ideologies, have been determined on the battlefields of the world and hence are not for our discussion or debate. Nor is it for us here to meet, representing as we do a majority of the people of the earth, in a spirit of distrust, malice or hatred.

"But rather it is for us, both victors and vanquished, to rise to that higher dignity which alone befits the sacred purposes we are about to serve, committing all our people unreservedly to faithful compliance with the obligation they are here formally to assume."

He voiced his hope for a better world, "founded upon faith and understanding," a world "dedicated to the dignity of man."

"As Supreme Commander for the Allied Powers," he concluded, "I announce it my firm purpose, in the tradition of the countries I represent, to proceed in the discharge of my responsibilities with justice and tolerance, while taking all necessary dispositions to insure that the terms of surrender are fully, promptly, and faithfully complied with."

With a stern gesture he invited the Japanese delegates to sign the instrument of surrender.

It was a painful moment for the Japanese. Foreign Minister Mamoru Shigemitsu hobbled forward on an artificial leg. Embarrassed, he fumbled nervously with his pen while he sought the proper line for his signature.

"Show him where to sign!" MacArthur snapped to General Sutherland.

At eight minutes past nine MacArthur formally accepted the Japanese capitulation by affixing his signature to the Instrument of Surrender as Supreme Commander for the Allied Powers.

Beginning with Admiral Nimitz, the United States Representative, all of the Allied representatives signed in turn. While they were signing, the sun broke through the clouds as though to light the dawning of a new era of peace.

As the last signature was drying on the Instrument of Surrender, a steady drone of approaching aircraft engines swelled into a mighty roar. A massed flight of 450 planes swept over the *Missouri* in a final salute to victory . . . and a reminder to all present of America's inexhaustible might.

As the roar died away MacArthur stepped forward again.

"Let us pray that peace be now restored to the world," he said slowly, "and that God will preserve it always. These preceedings are now closed."

Ashore, MacArthur found waiting for him a heart-warming message from Secretary of War Henry Stimson.

"With the full realization of our Pacific victory," it read,

"I send my warmest greetings and congratulations to you, who have been its principal architect. . . ." It was a generous accolade from a great and discerning man.

On September 8, with Halsey and Eichelberger, MacArthur drove through the twenty-two miles of devastation which lay between Yokohama and Tokyo. Most of his staff accompanied him.

At the American Embassy an honor guard from the 1st Cavalry Division was drawn up to receive him. On the terrace a soldier stood waiting at the flagpole, holding the same flag which had flown over the Capitol in Washington on the day of Pearl Harbor, and over the *Missouri* during the surrender ceremony.

"General Eichelberger," MacArthur commanded, "have our country's flag unfurled, and in Tokyo's sun let it wave in its full glory as a symbol of hope for the oppressed and as a harbinger of victory for the right."

As the flag rose and its folds loosened in the breeze, a crescendo of bugles paid homage to the ending of a long journey. A journey from defeat to victory.

A few days later MacArthur returned to Atsugi to meet the plane which was bringing his wife and son to Japan. No armed escort accompanied him.

As they drove back to Tokyo, through open countryside and ruined residential districts, thousands of expressionless Japanese watched them pass.

"Isn't this rather dangerous?" Mrs. MacArthur asked.

"No," her husband replied casually, "not particularly."

It was time of parting with old friends. Admiral Halsey called on MacArthur to say good-by. He would always treasure MacArthur's parting words.

"When you leave the Pacific, Bill, it becomes just another ocean."

Under the Four-Power agreement of August 14, 1945, MacArthur's authority over the Japanese was virtually absolute:

"From the moment of surrender, the authority of the Emperor and the Japanese Government to rule the state will be subject to you . . . You will exercise supreme command over all land, sea, and air forces which may be allocated for enforcement in Japan of the surrender terms by the allied forces concerned." He was armed with a conqueror's powers in a land where none but a conqueror is respected.

Since August 2 troops had been unloading daily and taking post in various parts of Japan. At the same time demobilized soldiers and sailors crowded the trains. To avoid possible incidents, the Emperor gave direct orders to his subjects. According to MacArthur, he "ordered the people to abide by the terms of the surrender and to work toward regaining the trust and faith of the world. He stressed the need for coolness, self-discipline. . . . To the Japanese, this was a clear directive to work in peace. . . ." As a result lone Americans could travel to remote places in complete safety.

MacArthur plunged immediately into the role of benevolent dictator of a nation of eighty million people. It was a strange task, and he had no precedents to guide him. He was on his own.

For the Japanese, revolutionary changes lay ahead. As rapidly as qualified officers and civilian specialists could be assigned to the tasks, he set out to destroy all military power and abolish police oppression; to decentralize the political

Arthur MacArthur, about
1899.

General Arthur MacArthur (foreground)
reviewing troops, about 1904.

Douglas MacArthur
at the age of two . . .

. . . and thirteen.

Cadet Douglas MacArthur, 1903.

West Point football team of 1902. Douglas MacArthur as manager, wearing Cadet gray.

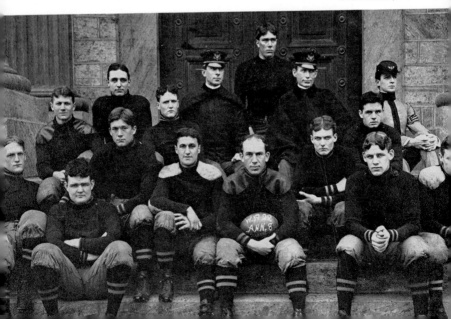

Lieutenant Douglas MacArthur on a survey trip, 1906.

United States Army Cavalry ascends Mexican foothills. Douglas MacArthur participated in the Villa Punitive Expedition.

MacArthur (upper left) and
members of the 84th Infantry
Brigade staff, 42nd (Rainbow) Division, in Germany,
March, 1918.

MacArthur with General De-
Bazelaire and staff members,
attending maneuvers of the
42nd Division in Glonville,
France.

In Manila, 1929.

Taking the oath of office as Chief of Staff before the Judge Advocate General, Major General Edward A. Kreger, on November 12, 1930.

With Major General Richard Sutherland, Corregidor Tunnel, March, 1942.

Wading ashore at Leyte Island, October, 1944.

U. S. Army photographs

Inspecting the ruins of his former home in Manila, February, 1945.

The formal surrender ceremonies on board the *U.S.S. Missouri,* August 31, 1945. Standing behind MacArthur are Lieutenant General Jonathan Wainwright (foreground) and Lieutenant General A. E. Percival.

As Commander-in-Chief, UN Command, in Tokyo, January 26, 1951

a tour of the front lines Korea, February, 1951.

Addressing members of Congress, April 19, 1951.

Review in honor of General Douglas MacArthur at West Point, May 12, 1962.

power and create a structure of representative government; to enfranchise the women, to liberalize education, and to free all political prisoners; to liberate the farmer from serfdom by reapportioning feudal lands; to establish a free economy and a free labor movement; and to develop a free but responsible press.

Troops began the destruction of the arms relinquished by the demobilized forces. When the task was completed, ten thousand airplanes, three thousand tanks, ninety thousand field pieces, three million items of small arms, and one million tons of explosives had been scrapped or dumped at sea.

Ironically, while these armaments were being destroyed in good faith, those seized by the Russians, in Manchuria, were being stored to arm their Red Chinese and North Korean satellites.

The General Headquarters of the Supreme Commander for the Allied Powers (SCAP) were established in the Dai Ichi Building, Tokyo's finest office structure. From it, directives began to roll forth to the Japanese government and to the troops in the field.

Initially tasks were assigned through purely military channels. While the destruction of Japan's armaments was in progress, troops took charge of receiving and distributing emergency food supplies, which had been sent from the United States. They supervised the repatriation of more than six million soldiers and sailors, who were being returned to Japan. More than a million displaced Koreans, Chinese, and Ryukyuans—all slave laborers—were returned to their homes. Allied prisoners of war were freed, and cared for until they could be sent home.

As a highly specialized staff of experts in various fields—

mining, forestry, labor, government, finance, industry—began to function in Tokyo, a Military Government structure was created in the field to implement SCAP directives and plans.

An Eighth Army Military Government team was established in each of Japan's forty-seven prefectures to see that the directives were carried out. The commander of the team did not replace the local governor. He was purely an advisor . . . with police powers. These teams worked at the grass-roots level to see that MacArthur's intended reforms were actually made.

From the Emperor down, MacArthur was careful not to supplant any level of government. His mission was to reform the existing governmental structure, not to destroy it. He wanted Japan to remain Japanese, but with its people's eyes opened to new concepts.

The Japanese economy had been wrecked. Industries had been destroyed by bombing raids. Those remaining had no raw materials with which to convert to peacetime demands. There were no foreign markets. Widespread unemployment and near famine disheartened the people. Apathy destroyed the will to self-betterment. Sullen, shabby, hungry, they moved about as though in a state of shock.

The Military Government teams attacked the problems with imagination and skill. Slowly production rose to meet consumer needs. Rationing distributed the scanty food supplies equitably. Incentive goods and the new freedoms stirred apathetic workers to fresh endeavors. A new Japan, born of MacArthur's reforms and developed by Japanese toil and ingenuity, began to rise from the ashes of defeat and desperation.

Japan's war criminals were brought to justice. "Occupation" courts tried them. Some were acquitted. Others were condemned for their crimes, sometimes to suffer death. The trials were conducted fairly and not in a spirit of revenge.

MacArthur wanted no revenge. The day of conquest had passed. New tasks faced him. He wanted only to rebuild a shattered nation, and to strike archaic shackles from the minds of a repressed people. They would comprehend democracy only if it were presented to them in a democratic guise. Reform, not revenge, was his goal.

Gradually, as confidence in MacArthur restored faith and incentive, his reforms began to be felt throughout Japan. The women turned out in masses to vote. Large estates were broken up into small parcels of land and sold to poor farmers at fair prices. Financial reforms were instituted. Shinto was abolished as a state religion. The schools began to teach liberal ideals. Labor unions were formed. Free speech became an accepted part of daily life. The old Meiji Constitution was liberalized.

Despite his progress and the extent of his reforms, MacArthur's path had not been a smooth one. For example, he had hardly begun his new duties when pressures were put upon him to add the Emperor's name to the list of war criminals. Sternly he resisted them. He knew how little the Emperor had had to do with Japan's war policies, and it was already apparent to him that, by making use of the Emperor's authority, he would win the confidence of the Japanese people and their more willing cooperation.

Both in Washington and in New York, his refusal created storms of abuse. The Communist *Daily Worker* was particularly vicious in its attacks, and it was echoed in large segments of the liberal press. Columnists and broadcasters joined in the cry to hang Hirohito. Some of the Allies, notably the British and Russians, added their voices; but MacArthur was adamant. Even had he wished to be a party to so unjust an action, the folly of it would have deterred him.

Finally, when official Washington seemed to be yielding to the clamor, he pointed out that he would need at least a million additional troops to suppress the guerrilla warfare which would result. Official pressures were withdrawn.

It was a wise decision. When the Japanese people learned that he had protected the Emperor's life, they accepted him as one in whom they could repose complete trust. The Emperor became his ally in speeding his proposed reforms.

As one year passed and then another, and MacArthur's star was still seen to rise rather than to fall, the disappointment of his enemies found voice in many places. In Tokyo the Russians attempted to flout SCAP directives. In a blistering denunciation in the press, MacArthur scored General Derevyanko, the chief of the Russian Mission, and held him up to public scorn as "an inciter of disorder and violence in an otherwise orderly Japanese society." Derevyanko retreated as though struck by an iron hand. MacArthur had no more troubles with the Russians.

By 1949 Japanese affairs had progressed to the point where a peace treaty was in the making and plans to end military government were shaping up. Yet MacArthur's load was no lighter. Outside of Japan sinister events had begun to claim his attention. Encouraged by ardent champions in many parts of the world, Mao Tse-tung's Russian-armed legions were becoming a serious threat to the peace of China.

In December, 1945, immediately following his retirement

from active service, General Marshall had been sent to China as a special ambassador.

Before departing he had received detailed instructions from the State Department. Under them, Marshall was to lend his prestige to arranging for an end to the civil war in China; but the arrangements were to include drastic measures which would permanently affect Free China. The Nationalist government was to be opened to Mao and the Red Chinese Army was to be merged with the Nationalist forces.

The end was not long in coming. Understandably failing in his efforts to persuade Chiang to permit Communist influence in his government, Marshall proposed an embargo on the sale of arms to both sides. It was declared. American support of Chiang's efforts in China ended. And since the Red Chinese were armed by the Russians, who laughed at the embargo, Chiang and the remnants of his armies retreated to Formosa, one hundred miles off the China coast.

MacArthur watched the passing of Chiang with dismay. A staunch ally had fallen, and an almost unbroken front of Communism now faced Japan. One country alone remained free—South Korea; and for months MacArthur had watched with misgivings a Russian build-up of North Korean forces which could have but one purpose.

South Korea was outside of MacArthur's jurisdiction. Nevertheless, his intelligence sources had kept him informed of developments there. Repeatedly he had warned the authorities in Washington that a large-scale invasion was in preparation. His warnings were often ignored. The State Department did not even see fit to remove American citizens from its path.

In Japan, MacArthur watched the ominous build-up with

concern. His forces had been reduced to four under-strength divisions. Their occupation duties made combat training difficult to conduct. Regiments were each short a battalion; battalions were short a company . . . all in the interests of economy. The soldiers were largely postwar enlistees who had had no experience in battle. They were soft and they lacked discipline. Their arms were becoming obsolete. These things, the Russians knew.

15.

THE LANDING AT INCHON

✗ An arbitrary boundary separated North and South Korea. In 1945 it had been fixed at the 38th Parallel of latitude to designate zones in which American and Russian troops would receive the surrender of Japanese forces. It had not been intended as a permanent frontier. Nevertheless, the Russians had closed this arbitrary "border," and brain-washing, youth indoctrination, and bloody purges had transformed North Korea into a Russian satellite state.

The lifelong Korean patriot, Synghman Rhee, had returned from exile following the Japanese surrender. A Republic of South Korea was created, with him as its President. With American arms and advisory assistance, an army came into being. But it matched neither in strength nor in armaments the powerful, Russian-trained North Korean forces.

The State Department which, since 1948, had controlled South Korean affairs, had limited South Korea's arms to light weapons "to prevent the South Koreans from attacking North Korea."

For months MacArthur had watched events in Korea with misgivings. Early on Sunday morning, June 25, 1950, the telephone awakened him.

"General," he was informed, "a dispatch from Seoul has advised us that the North Koreans have crossed the 38th Parallel in force."

"Call me as the situation develops," MacArthur instructed.

He rose and paced the floor, deep in thought. The news was shocking, but he was not surprised. Even though Korea lay outside of his zone of responsibility, he had kept himself fully informed of events there. During the preceding six months he had sent 417 intelligence summaries to Washington. They had revealed in detail the ominous build-up of North Korean forces along the 38th Parallel.

There were other sources of information. Only a few days before, John Foster Dulles had visited Korea as the personal representative of Secretary of State Dean Acheson. He had been fully informed of the threat. Yet, in a few days, MacArthur would learn that official Washington had been shocked by the unexpected event.

What stand would the President take, MacArthur wondered. Plans for the defense of Asia, lately revised by the Joint Chiefs of Staff, assumed that Korea would not be defended. Yet Dulles had implied to the members of the South Korean legislature that America would defend Korea if attacked.

For the moment MacArthur's sole responsibility was for

the evacuation of some two thousand Americans from Korea, if and when the Ambassador requested it. Plans had already been prepared. That task accomplished, would the President consider his whole duty done? The answer came quickly.

At the President's request, the Security Council of the United Nations met that afternoon. Fortunately the Russians were boycotting the Council, so a resolution introduced by the United States was adopted without delay. It called for an immediate cessation of hostilities, for the withdrawal of the North Korean forces, and for all members of the Council to aid in the execution of the resolution.

Instinctively a fighter, President Truman seized upon the measure as authority to extend immediate military assistance to South Korea. He ordered MacArthur to use the Navy and the Air Force to assist in its defense. He assigned the Seventh Fleet to MacArthur's command to defend Chiang Kai-shek's forces on Formosa from Communist attack. Unfortunately he also ordered that it was to prevent Chiang from raiding the mainland.

Immediately MacArthur's plan for the evacuation of the Americans—men, women, and children—from Korea was put into effect. Its success elicited high praise, both from Ambassador Muccio and from the Joint Chiefs of Staff.

Far-reaching problems faced MacArthur . . . and a task whose magnitude he understood, but which obviously no one in Washington had begun to comprehend.

Would sea and air support be enough to enable the South Koreans to hold their own? He doubted it. There was but one way to find the answer. He would go and see for himself.

It was raining on the morning of June 29 when, with a party of staff members and correspondents, he took off for

Korea in the unarmed *Bataan*. The news had been discouraging. Seoul had fallen, and the government had retreated to Taejon, miles to the south.

The *Bataan* landed at Suwon in the smoke of two transports which had just been strafed by enemy planes. The field had been under attack since dawn, so MacArthur sent the *Bataan* back to Tokyo. It was to return at five o'clock.

MacArthur listened intently as Brigadier General John H. Church explained the alarming situation. When Church had finished, he stood up and said, "Let's go to the front and have a look."

Even though the front had disintegrated, and enemy tanks and foot columns were dangerously near, they made their way through the backwash of the defeated South Koreans to the bank of the Han River, at which most of the enemy had been checked for the moment by destroyed bridges.

They climbed to the top of a hill which gave them a commanding view. In the distance smoke rose from ruined Seoul. Enemy fire from across the river harassed the retreating troops. Death and destruction lay all around them. Pitiful refugees, carrying their remaining possessions, clogged the roads, with terror-stricken children clutching at their hands and garments.

For a while MacArthur stood on the hilltop, silently assessing the extent of the disaster. It was as he had feared. The South Korean forces had dissolved into unmanageable mobs. There was nothing to stop the enemy advance except destroyed bridges, and an occasional brave stand at a favorable point by a still intact South Korean unit. It was obvious that American ground troops must be used to stem the Red tide.

It was a repetition of Bataan. Neglect, and unrealistic evaluations of the enemy's intentions, had again set the stage for defeat. Again he had been given the task of leading a forlorn hope. Again his soldiers would die because of other men's failures.

Nevertheless, his mind was busily at work on the problem of restoring a fighting front. It was busy, too, planning the only strategy which could snatch victory from defeat.

Back at the temporary headquarters, President Rhee was waiting to see MacArthur. They had known each other since before World War I, when Rhee was a student in Washington. Each admired the other's devotion to his chosen duty.

Aerial combats raged overhead, and enemy planes strafed the area, as they discussed the grim situation.

Six North Korean infantry divisions had invaded South Korea, spearheaded by some hundred Russian tanks. Heavy artillery reinforced them.

Four lightly armed ROK (Republic of Korea) divisions, without tanks or heavy artillery, had tried to oppose them. They had been swept away as leaves before a strong wind.

At five o'clock the *Bataan* landed and her passengers hastened aboard. Only a few minutes before the field had been bombed and strafed. When they were airborne, and well beyond the range of enemy fighters, all sighed with relief ... all except MacArthur. Pencil in hand, he was already drafting his recommendations to the Joint Chiefs of Staff.

It was a grim message. In it MacArthur outlined the full extent of the disaster and stressed the need for American ground troops. He requested authority to employ a regimental combat team immediately, and to prepare two divisions of his troops in Japan to follow. Without the full utilization of air, sea, and ground forces, he warned, efforts to stop the Red advance might be doomed to failure.

Within twenty-four hours the President assented, and a few token troops were on the way. It was a strategy of desperation which violated every rule of war, but it was based upon MacArthur's knowledge of the Oriental mind. He was sure that the mere sight of American troops would cause the North Korean commander to halt while he assessed the strength of the American "forces." It would gain valuable time.

These token troops established road blocks and fought desperately to halt the enemy advance. Their presence served MacArthur's purpose. The enemy commander halted his columns and spent hours bringing heavy artillery forward. Puzzled by the unexpected American appearance, he redeployed all of his forces to meet a counterattack.

MacArthur had won the first round of what General Whitney later described as a "duel of nerve and wit." It gave him time to move reinforcements forward to replace the sadly decimated little advance force whose presence had halted the enemy. A desperate gamble had paid off, but at the sacrifice of brave men—victims of American economy.

Ten days passed before the Communist commander realized that he had been tricked. Those ten days enabled MacArthur to bring in the rest of Major General William F. Dean's 24th Division to delay the enemy until the 25th Division and the 1st Cavalry Division arrived. Dean fought a desperate series of isolated engagements. Finally he was captured and the 24th Division almost destroyed; but not until he had made the enemy's renewed advance costly and slow, and reinspired the South Korean forces to fresh efforts.

During these fateful days MacArthur established Eighth Army headquarters in Korea. In the Eighth Army's commander, Lieutenant General Walton H. Walker, he had a fighting leader upon whom he could rely.

At the port of Pusan, on Korea's southeast coast, Major General Crump Garvin quickly brought order out of the chaos created by the shiploads of supplies and equipment which, rushed from Japan, were being dumped hastily ashore.

With a speed perhaps never matched in a mobilization toward a battlefield, the Eighth Army reached Korea—three under-strength divisions, with neither adequate firepower nor more than a sprinkling of battle-wise men. MacArthur still had neither the men nor the weapons to match those arrayed against him. He was heavily outnumbered, and the North Koreans were lavishly equipped with the latest Russian arms. Only in the air were the North Koreans matched in planes and outclassed in men. They were soon cleared from the skies.

On July 7 MacArthur requested reinforcements. He explained to the Joint Chiefs of Staff that he faced "an aggressive and well-trained professional army . . . operating under top-level guidance." He was planning ahead. Already he was intent upon the strategy which he had planned on the hilltop ten days before.

This estimate of his needs, he reminded the Joint Chiefs of Staff, was based solely on requirements to defeat the North Koreans. Should Russia or Red China intervene, he warned them, "a new situation would develop which is not predictable now."

His request for reinforcements was denied. Europe still

came first, even though the up-to-strength, fully equipped, finely tempered combat divisions there were doing nothing but peacetime duties. Korea, like Bataan, must provide for its own survival.

On the 8th MacArthur was appointed Commander-in-Chief of the United Nations Forces in Korea. Some of the member nations were sending at least token forces to Korea to augment the American troops there.

Although South Korea was not a member of the United Nations, President Rhee gave MacArthur complete command over his country's forces.

MacArthur made revolutionary use of this welcome reservoir of manpower. Five of the ROK divisions were back in action, fighting under American supervision. Others were still disorganized, leaving thousands of soldiers unassigned. Walker's three under-strength divisions were suffering battle losses. So MacArthur integrated the South Korean soldiers into Walker's ranks.

There was immediate resentment and skepticism, but MacArthur squelched all opposition. The ROK's worked hard and learned fast, and they strove to outdo their mentors in skill and daring. The language difficulty disappeared quickly. In a short time the Americans accepted their new charges and saw that they were treated fairly in all matters.

The ROK's were like men reborn. Their shame over the terrible defeat in June was forgotten. They were transformed from dejected failures into proud and confident soldiers.

MacArthur's ingenious solution to his replacement problem enabled him to prevent possible disaster. It doubled Walker's firepower and gave him a means of replacing his day-to-day losses.

The Eighth Army had saved South Korea from being completely overrun. The enemy had lost his greatest opportunity.

"He has had his great chance," MacArthur stated, "but failed to exploit it. We are now in Korea in force and, with God's help, we are here to stay."

To protect the growing base at Pusan, a defense perimeter had been established behind the Naktong River, with each flank resting on the sea. Although he could hang on indefinitely, to MacArthur hanging on was tantamount to defeat. He planned to land a force at Inchon, on the opposite coast, to sever the enemy's communications and attack him from the rear.

The enemy was experiencing the same frustration that Homma had felt on Bataan. Had they been better informed, they might have remembered Hollandia and prepared for the daring plan that MacArthur had conceived that first day in Korea.

On the 23rd he submitted his plan. Already his staff was deeply engrossed in developing the myriad details. Not that he felt confident of approval. Months earlier General Omar Bradley, Chairman of the Joint Chiefs of Staff, had declared that amphibious operations were outdated. If the plan were vetoed, the Eighth Army was doomed to a hopeless defense . . . or to be committed to a terrible blood bath of frontal assaults, shocking to MacArthur but which in Europe had been routine.

"Operation planned," his message explained, "is amphibious landing in rear of enemy lines in conjunction with attack from south by Eighth Army. I am firmly convinced that strong effort behind his front will sever his main lines of communication and enable us to deliver a decisive blow. . . ."

For three weeks he heard nothing. Then he received word that General J. Lawton Collins, Army Chief of Staff, and Admiral Forrest Sherman, Chief of Naval Operations, were en route to Tokyo to discuss the plan with him.

On August 23 the most important conference of the Korean War was held in the Dai Ichi Building. MacArthur, Collins, Sherman; Marine Corps Commandant Lemuel Shepherd, Admirals Turner Joy and Arthur Struble; Major General Edward M. Almond, who would command the X Corps on the landing; a galaxy of staff officers and aides.

MacArthur invited the Navy to present its case first. It was a gloomy picture. Tide and terrain, the briefing officer argued, made a landing at Inchon extremely hazardous. The rise and fall of the tide was one of the greatest in the world. On the projected date it would be thirty feet. "Flying Fish Channel," through which the tides raced, was narrow, winding, and easily mined. A sunken ship would block it. High tide would come at 6:59 in the morning and at 7:19 in the evening, thirty-five minutes after sunset.

There would be little time to land troops, secure a beachhead, and bring in supplies before the ebb tide stopped all operations. Further, the landing would have to be made in the city, where every building offered concealment for the defenders. Summing up the Navy's objections, Admiral Sherman said, "If every possible geographical and naval handicap were listed, Inchon has 'em all."

Collins then presented the Army's objections. Inchon, the Army believed, was too far in the rear of the present battle area to have the necessary effect upon the enemy. It was doubted that, even if he reached Seoul, MacArthur could make contact with Walker. Further, MacArthur might find overwhelming enemy forces in the Seoul area.

Patiently MacArthur heard them out. When they had finished, he remained silent for a moment. Tension rose in the room as the group wondered how he meant to meet all of the objections.

When he spoke, it was in a casual, confident tone.

"The very arguments you have made as to the impracticabilities involved," he said, "will tend to insure for me the element of surprise. The enemy commander will reason that no one would be so brash as to make such an attempt. Surprise is the most vital element for success in modern war."

He was convinced that the enemy had neglected to defend Inchon. They were too heavily committed against Walker's forces. As for the Navy's objections, the handicaps were substantial but they were not insuperable. The Navy's vast experience in amphibious landings gave him complete confidence in their abilities.

The enemy's vulnerability lay in his supply lines, he explained. These could be severed completely at Seoul, where they all centered. Seoul could be reached only through Inchon. With their communications cut, supplies would soon be exhausted and the enemy would have to retreat. Hungry and disorganized, they could easily be overpowered by our well-supplied forces.

"The only alternative to a stroke such as I propose would be the continuation of the savage sacrifice we are making at Pusan, with no hope of relief in sight. Are you content," he asked them, "to let our troops stay in that bloody perimeter like beef cattle in the slaughterhouse? Who would take the responsibility for such a tragedy? Certainly, I will not!

"The prestige of the Western world hangs in the balance," he went on feelingly. "Oriental millions are watching. Here in Asia is where the Communist conspirators have elected to make their play for global conquest. The test is not in Berlin. It is here and now—in South Korea. Here we fight Europe's war with arms, while there it is confined to words. If we lose the war to Communism in Asia, the fate of Europe will be gravely jeopardized. Win it, and Europe will stay free!"

Nothing more was said. But six days later he received the approval of the Joint Chiefs of Staff. *on Aug 29*.

and As he had predicted, the landing was a complete surprise. *on Sept 15 1950* The Navy's timing was perfect, and the Marines landed swiftly and without a single loss. When they had secured the beachhead, MacArthur turned to the navy and marine officers who stood with him on the bridge of the flagship and said to them simply, "Well done!"

Almond's X Corps moved swiftly inland toward fixed objectives. One column set out toward Seoul, to cut the enemy's communications. Another moved toward Pusan.

Within three days the enemy fire slackened along Walker's front. Immediately he launched an attack. Caught between Walker and Almond, the Reds broke completely. Whole units disintegrated and fled, abandoning arms and equipment. Trapped, 130,000 prisoners fell into MacArthur's hands. He had snatched victory from near defeat. A few days of mopping up, and South Korea would be free.

On the 29th, two weeks after the landing at Inchon, MacArthur flew to Seoul to officiate at a civil ceremony. In a few simple words he handed the seat of his government back to President Rhee. It was a touching moment. When it was over, he said:

"In humble and devout manifestation of gratitude to Almighty God for bringing this decisive victory to our arms, I ask that all present rise and join me in reciting the Lord's Prayer."

Loosened by the wind, particles of glass from the shattered roof fell among the crowd as it murmured in unison, "Thine is the Kingdom, the Power and the Glory, for ever and ever. Amen."

In July, MacArthur informed the Joint Chiefs of Staff that, on the 31st, he planned to visit Formosa with a group of staff officers to analyze its defense potential. Conflicting stories had reached him. As always, he preferred to see for himself.

Despite their close relationship as allies, MacArthur and Chiang had never met. He was received cordially, and spent a fruitful day in gaining firsthand knowledge of the local military situation.

It had not occurred to MacArthur that his visit could be construed as political in nature. Since it was a routine matter, and there was nothing secret about it, he made an open statement to the press in Tokyo the next day which confirmed the strictly military nature of the journey.

"Arrangements have been completed," he announced, "for effective coordination between the American forces under my command and those of the Chinese government. It has been a great pleasure to me to meet my old comrade-in-arms of the last war, Generalissimo Chiang Kai-shek. His indomitable determination to resist Communist domination arouses my sincere admiration. His determination parallels the common interests and purpose of Americans, that all people in the Pacific area shall be free, not slaves."

Newspapers flayed MacArthur for his eulogy of America's

faithful ally, Chiang. Some columnists and commentators introduced hints of political ambitions, and of interference in State Department affairs.

Shortly some of the rumors became so serious that they began to gain world-wide attention. And yet no one in Washington made any attempt to set the situation straight.

Even the President remained silent. Later MacArthur was told that his notification of his intended visit to Formosa had been sent to the State Department, but that evidently it had been stopped there. It had been easy, apparently, to suggest to Mr. Truman that MacArthur had left Japan and visited Formosa without proper notification to the Joint Chiefs of Staff.

At any rate, no matter what the cause, this was the opening of a serious breach in the cordial relationship which had existed between the President and General MacArthur.

16.

NO SUBSTITUTE FOR VICTORY

✗   In October, MacArthur was ordered to complete the destruction of the North Korean armed forces. He was authorized to conduct military operations north of the 38th Parallel, but he was directed that "under no circumstances, however, will your forces [which included aircraft] cross the Manchurian or U.S.S.R. borders of Korea. . . ."

The effect of this restriction upon MacArthur's use of his superior air capabilities was to provide the enemy with what the General described as "privileged sanctuaries." In them, the enemy could bring up reinforcements safely. From them, he could launch devastating attacks without fear of reprisal.

Swiftly the victorious Eighth Army fought its way forward to clear North Korea of enemy forces. Resistance stiffened as they moved deep into enemy territory, but they pressed on. On their right, separated from Walker's greater force by the massive ridges which bisect the Korean peninsula, Almond's X Corps moved up the east coast.

As Walker and Almond moved forward, their movements coordinated by MacArthur's headquarters, MacArthur learned that large bodies of Red Chinese troops, including Lin-piao's veteran Fourth Army, were moving toward the Yalu. Freed from guarding China's long coast line by the President's policy of "containing" Chiang with the Seventh Fleet, these masses posed a new threat. If they were launched across the Yalu, the United Nations forces would be in serious jeopardy.

It was well within MacArthur's power to defeat them. Their bases and concentration areas were vulnerable to air assaults. But so long as he was restricted from destroying these "privileged sanctuaries," he would be forced either to retreat or to engage overwhelmingly superior numbers with his strongest hand—his air power—tightly tied. Yet he was not unduly worried. It never occurred to him that, once the lives of his soldiers and the prestige of his country were at stake, those restrictions would not be lifted.

On October 12 MacArthur was informed that the President wished to meet him at Wake Island on the 15th.

When the President's plane arrived, MacArthur was waiting. He had never met Mr. Truman, but he had admired his fighting qualities and appreciated the friendly regard in which the President appeared to hold him.

He had been puzzled at the purpose of the meeting. His views on every pertinent subject were already well known in Washington. He had been reluctant to leave Tokyo at this critical time; but he realized that the President, too, was taking time from his duties during a sensitive period, so the reason must be an important one.

When Mr. Truman descended from his plane, MacArthur greeted him warmly. As they shook hands, the President said, "I've been a long time meeting you, General."

"I hope that it won't be so long next time," MacArthur replied. Neither was aware that there would never be another meeting.

They retired to a Quonset hut and talked privately for half an hour. The talk was routine. When they joined the others, in the island's administration building, the President had an agenda on a small piece of paper. His first statement amazed MacArthur.

"General MacArthur and I have talked fully about Formosa," he stated. "We are in complete agreement."

Beginning with Korea, several subjects had been discussed, but these did not include Formosa. On each, MacArthur's views were requested. When he had given them, the President invariably concurred.

Finally he had asked MacArthur, "What are the chances for Chinese or Soviet interference?" It was a loaded question but, having sensed no reason to be wary of it, MacArthur answered frankly.

Since his viewpoint was based solely upon military considerations, he pointed out that his answer would be purely speculative. But since neither the Defense Department, the State Department, nor the Central Intelligence Agency had given him any reason to believe otherwise, his present guess would be: "Very little."

Neither the President, General Bradley, nor any of the

other high officials present—including the State Department's Far Eastern Chief, Dean Rusk—offered a contrary opinion, so MacArthur assumed that his views had been accepted.

At this point Douglas MacArthur committed the gravest error of his career. He assumed too much, trusted too much. He failed to ask the President, in the presence of witnesses, if he would be allowed to use his air power to smash a Red Chinese attack. The answer—or the lack of one—might well have put him on his guard and saved the United Nations forces in North Korea from near disaster.

Then, to MacArthur's complete surprise, the President awarded him an Oak Leaf Cluster to his Distinguished Service Medal, his fifth award of that honor. The citation lauded MacArthur so highly that no one who heard it could have suspected that, when asked years later if he had ever repented relieving MacArthur, the by then ex-President snapped, "I repent that I didn't do it two years sooner."

Since he had been told nothing to the contrary, MacArthur left Wake Island sure that the bulk of his victorious troops would be back in Japan by Christmas, leaving only security forces along the Republic of Korea's re-established north boundary. Bradley had even discussed withdrawing at least a division from Korea for employment in Europe.

The President had seemed warm and friendly. Apparently he approved of the conduct of affairs in Korea. Settled back in his seat, MacArthur relaxed as the *Bataan* winged its way home. After a time he slept.

He would have been coldly awake had he known what events were shaping up in the "privileged sanctuaries" on the Manchurian banks of the Yalu . . . and what secret assurances had determined the Red Chinese course. It would have enabled him to meet a new threat in a far different manner. But he did not begin to suspect these things until his army was reeling back from the Yalu in defeat and his hands remained tied. By then it was too late.

Five days later MacArthur watched from his plane as the 187th Regimental Combat Team jumped behind the enemy's lines north of Pyongyang, the North Korean capital, to cut off the enemy's retreat while Walker entered the city. The fall of Pyongyang symbolized the destruction of the North Korean government. In a short time its last organized forces would be defeated and dispersed.

MacArthur was jubilant. Victory appeared to be in sight. He had yet to learn that, secretly, approximately five thousand Red Chinese troops had crossed the Yalu and moved into hidden positions beyond Walker's flank.

On the 26th ROK forces reached the Yalu but were forced to retire. On Walker's left the 24th Division met strong resistance as it neared Shinuiju, where the North Korean government had fled.

On the 30th Chinese prisoners were taken near Chongin, on the east coast. Although some were in Red uniform, all claimed to be volunteers fighting with the North Koreans.

Despite these indications of Red Chinese infiltration, MacArthur received the approval of the Joint Chiefs of Staff to continue to push forward. He was eager to deliver the *coup de grâce* before winter set in and before the North Koreans could be reinforced strongly with Red Chinese "volunteers."

A few days later, General Ho Shai-lai, the Nationalist Chinese Ambassador in Tokyo, warned MacArthur that Nationalist intelligence sources had confirmed rumors that Red Chinese regular forces had entered North Korea in force. It was believed that the Reds had received assurance that, no matter what the provocation, their "sanctuaries" would not be disturbed.

MacArthur could not understand this, except for one factor. In Europe, the Russians were, in his opinion, running a gigantic bluff with incredible success. Even though all of their military dispositions were defensive, their saber rattling had shaped the military policies of the United States. The old "Europe first" fixation of World War II days was again endangering American security in the Pacific. Apparently the Administration had ceased to think in terms of what America *could* do; it grieved MacArthur that the most powerful nation on earth had been reduced to policies of appeasement—policies based on what Russia might possibly do.

He received other chilling information. His advancing forces had met a series of sharp counterblows; and interrogations of prisoners revealed that an estimated three divisions of Red Chinese troops were opposing the United Nations forces.

Was it, MacArthur asked himself, a Red bluff, intended to warn him away from the Manchurian border? Was it a reconnaissance in force, to determine his strength and intentions? Or was it the forerunner of a full scale intervention by the Red Chinese?

Since Washington appeared to be unconcerned as to the possibility of such a move, the latter supposition appeared to be improbable. The others were not important. It appeared to be most likely that these units had been "volunteered" by Mao to stiffen Korean resistance without involving Red China formally.

Whatever the reason for their presence, MacArthur had no

intention of abandoning his mission of clearing Korea of enemy forces. It appeared that the Joint Chiefs of Staff had reached similar conclusions. Earlier MacArthur had been directed that, should the Red Chinese intervene, he should go on the defensive and request further instructions. A new directive now gave him broader authority.

"Hereafter," he was instructed, "in the event of the open or covert employment anywhere in Korea of major Chinese Communist units, without prior announcement, you should continue the action as long as, in your judgment, action by forces now under your control offers a reasonable chance of success."

MacArthur was elated. The directive appeared to assure him that, should grave danger develop, he would be permitted to use his air power to meet it. His elation was short-lived.

In keeping with his broader authority, he ordered Stratemeyer to bomb the Yalu bridges. This would stop the flow of reinforcements and supplies to both enemies. Routinely he notified the Joint Chiefs of Staff of his decision.

Immediately he received instructions to countermand his order and to "postpone all bombing of targets within five miles of the Manchurian border until further notice." The Red's "privileged sanctuaries" had been extended five miles into Korea.

Astonished, MacArthur canceled his orders and sent a reply. In it, he pointed out that the only way to stop heavy reinforcements from crossing the Yalu was to destroy the bridges.

"I can accept the instructions rescinding my orders only under the gravest protest," he stated, "as I feel that they might well result in a calamity of gravest proportions, for which I could not accept the responsibility. Urgently request reconsideration of your decision, or that the matter be brought to the attention of the President."

The result was a modification of the order. He was permitted to bomb the "Korea end of the bridges," a half-measure which placed Stratemeyer's bombers at a costly disadvantage.

Upon learning some of the air losses caused by this kind of policy, MacArthur exploded to his staff: "For the first time in military history, a commander has been denied the use of his military power to safeguard the lives of his soldiers and the safety of his army."

Even when the United Nations forces were fighting for their lives, the policy remained unaltered. The bridges stood. Because of them, the Reds were able to pit hundreds of thousands of men against MacArthur's relatively small forces, and to move supplies forward with impunity.

The British recommended giving Red China a large slice of North Korea as a "buffer area." MacArthur made a fervent plea against this proposed appeasement.

"To give up a portion of North Korea to the aggression of the Red Chinese Communists would be the greatest defeat of the Free World in recent times. Indeed, to yield to so immoral a proposition would bankrupt our leadership and influence in Asia. . . . I recommend with all the earnestness that I possess that there be no weakening at this critical moment and that we press on to complete victory."

During November signs pointed dangerously toward a full-scale Red Chinese intervention. Yet if either the State

Department or the Central Intelligence Agency had detected signs of such an intent, the information was not passed on.

If no greater intervention was intended, he was pursuing the proper course in pushing forward to smash the last enemy forces. Actually, he had no alternative. He could not abandon his mission and retreat, merely in the face of possibilities. But in case he should be wrong, and overwhelming forces attempted to entrap him, he prepared plans which would enable his forces to disengage and withdraw safely. These plans were approved by the Joint Chiefs of Staff.

Safe from attack, Chinese Communists were pouring across the bridges which American policy had preserved for them. More than two hundred thousand had already crossed and were deployed in concealed areas. Had the bridges been destroyed, the Yalu would have held them back.

On November 24 MacArthur flew to Eighth Army headquarters. That afternoon, airborne for the return to Tokyo, he ordered his pilot to fly up the Yalu from its mouth. He wanted to study the terrain and look for enemy activity. Since the plane was unarmed and had but a small fighter escort, he was urged to put on a parachute.

"You gentlemen wear them if you care to do so," he said, "but I'll stick with the plane."

As they followed the river at an altitude of five thousand feet, MacArthur studied the ground. Although there was nothing to indicate movements of troops or trains, the intermittent snow storms could well have covered all signs. To the eye, it was an empty and forbidding land; yet the forests hid thousands upon thousands of the enemy.

On the 26th the Red Chinese struck. Massive attacks developed all along the icy miles of the Eighth Army front.

Keyed up for days in anticipation of such a move, the troops were prepared to meet them. They met the assaults in skillfully prepared positions and threw them back with bloody losses, until on the right the ROK's broke under the constant hammering and exposed the Eighth Army's right flank to encirclement.

Sadly MacArthur informed the Joint Chiefs of Staff of the new war in which the United Nations were now engaged.

On the east, separated by the rugged mountain range, the X Corps was not at first attacked. The 1st Marine Division, supported by the 7th Division, was pushed to the west to strike the rear of the attackers and disrupt their communications. But more masses of Chinese poured across the bridges and almost trapped them before they could withdraw.

It was obvious to MacArthur that only with luck could he stem the Red tide with the troops then in Korea, unless he was permitted to destroy the Yalu bridges and the enemy's "sanctuaries."

He needed reinforcements. In Formosa thirty-three thousand veteran troops were available for the asking—troops eager to settle old scores with the Reds. Washington did not permit MacArthur to accept them. It was said that the British, who had only a token force in Korea, could not allow themselves to be identified with the Nationalists.

Permission to use his air power was still denied MacArthur, and with an air of finality which dismayed him. It appeared that he was engaged in the first war in American history in which the nation seemed to have interests on both sides.

His visits to the front angered him: the biting cold intensified the hardships the soldiers were enduring, and these hardships were doubled by the lack of reinforcements and by the ease with which the enemy could bring up new masses to replace their heavy losses. There was no rest and, as Mac-Arthur knew, no hope of victory unless American policies were changed.

First-rate leadership and heroic fighting had stabilized the front in the Pyongyang area. Temporarily at least the Chinese were stopped. But the effort had been costly and the outlook was discouraging. Morale suffered as the men began to realize that they were being sacrificed for obscure reasons.

In Japan the people were disturbed. They knew that Mac-Arthur had the means to smash the enemy and restore Korea to its people. Obviously, mysterious forces were at work. How might it affect them?

"Why do you fight," they asked American friends, "if you do not want to win?" There was no rational answer.

On December 23 General Walker was killed in an accident. To MacArthur, it was a sad blow. "Johnnie" Walker had been a tower of strength during these desperate months. A few days later, at MacArthur's request, Lieutenant General Mathew B. Ridgway assumed command of the doggedly determined Eighth Army. It was a happy choice. His commanding personality, and his own splendid combat record, soon won the confidence of these war-wise men.

Although few people suspected it, MacArthur's days as Supreme Commander for the Allied Powers were numbered.

His insistence that current policies were compromising America's prestige in the Far East, and his continued pleas for the removal of the restrictions which had condemned his troops to slow destruction, could not have been made more clear.

However, administration officials and others in Washington felt otherwise.

Some people charged that MacArthur had allowed himself to be surprised. He had moved forward without the approval of the Joint Chiefs of Staff.

Yet, all over America, there were other, far differing views. Many people saw in MacArthur their best hope of salvaging victory from defeat. Though largely unorganized, these people were definitely there, as the President learned later.

Though there are many opinions on the subject, one group points out that President Truman's course of action with MacArthur seems to have been based on political expediency.

In July, 1951, three months after MacArthur had departed for home, an elderly Japanese of high standing in the old hierarchy was asked his opinion as to the reason for General MacArthur's relief. Without hesitation, he replied:

"Ah! You have national election in your country next year. General MacArthur make President Truman look very bad. So he go home."

How close was he to the truth? Some years later a well-known Washington figure revealed confidentially the political factors which he alleged brought the ouster.

In 1948 MacArthur had permitted his name to be used in the Wisconsin Republican primary. It was strictly a trial balloon, and his support had not been impressive. However, many observers felt that personal appearances would have made a strong difference. The war had been over for three years, and the man in the street knew little of MacArthur's accomplishments in Japan.

In 1950 the situation had changed. Again his name was well-known. Again his victories, his over-all achievement,

had stirred the American imagination. Political strategists—
and President Truman was one of the most accomplished—
watched reactions closely.

On December 6, 1950, a presidential directive required
the clearance of MacArthur's speeches, press releases, and
other statements through censoring hands. He observed the
directive with scrupulous care.

Probably the single most important political event, however, took place many weeks later. In a private letter, Congressman Joseph W. Martin sought MacArthur's views con-
cerning America's position in Asia. He enclosed a speech
which he had delivered in which he had stressed the terrible
price should America fail to win in Korea.

"I think it is imperative," his letter read, "... that the
forces of Generalissimo Chiang Kai-shek on Formosa be
employed in opening a second front to relieve pressure on
our forces in Korea...."

Earlier MacArthur had written a personal note to General
Collins, urging that Nationalist Chinese troops be used. Now,
in his reply to Martin—intended solely for his private information—he concurred heartily with the Congressman's views.

"My views and recommendations," he wrote, "... have
been submitted to Washington in most complete detail. Your
view with respect to the utilization of the Chinese forces on
Formosa is in conflict with neither logic nor tradition. As you
pointed out, we must win. There is no substitute for victory."

It had always been the Army's policy that queries from
Members of Congress must be answered frankly and
promptly, which MacArthur did. And he had expressed no
view that was not already known.

Without consulting MacArthur, Martin read the reply on

the floor of the House. Within a few minutes Mr. Truman had been informed of it, and his actions were swift indeed.

Inadvertently Martin had brought the whole affair to a crisis: the heroic General and the question of the chain of command, his accomplishments, and his necessary obedience to the Commander-in-Chief were seized upon by hostile critics.

Immediately MacArthur was relieved of his several commands. He was ordered home.

17.

OLD SOLDIERS NEVER DIE

✗ It had rained all night. In the early afternoon of April 11, 1951, the rain was still falling intermittently on the roof of the American Embassy in Tokyo, where the MacArthurs had lived since the beginning of the Occupation.

Outside there was a damp chill in the air. It was raw for April, and the streets were less crowded than usual. Only at the Dai Ichi Building, opposite the Imperial Palace, were the usual crowds formed, the rain spilling from their umbrellas, to watch for the General's return from lunch. It was a daily affair, and the audience never appeared to dwindle.

Inside the Embassy, in the warmth of a cheerful room, the MacArthurs chatted pleasantly with their luncheon guests, unaware that a special news bulletin had startled the entire world.

"The President," the bulletin read, "has just removed General MacArthur from his Far Eastern and Korean commands and from direction of the occupation of Japan."

MacArthur was talking when his wife, from her end of the table, looked over his shoulder and saw in the doorway the anguished face of one of his aides, Colonel Sidney L. Huff. Quietly she excused herself and left the table.

There were tears in Huff's eyes as he told her the news—news which no one in authority had broken to MacArthur before it was given to the world. Fifty years of service and great achievement had prepared him for nothing like this.

There were tears in Jean MacArthur's eyes, too, as she returned to the table. With a word of apology to the others, she leaned down and whispered the news to her husband.

His face froze, but no trace of emotion betrayed the shock. In a moment the puzzled luncheon guests heard him say gently, "Jeannie, we're going home at last."

MacArthur wasted no time in reflection. There was too much to be done. At his headquarters cables soon confirmed the radio announcement. The relief from command was "effective at once," an unprecedented slap at a man who had served with distinction through three wars, who had held the highest military posts at his country's command, and who was the nation's most decorated officer for bravery in battle.

No one questioned Mr. Truman's right, as President, to relieve him; but the nature of his act outraged the sensibilities of Americans and Orientals alike, and led millions to question his motives.

The Japanese were shocked. "Why," they asked, "does the greatest nation on earth thus treat its most distinguished son?" "Macassa Gensui" had become the rock of their faith.

Without him, what would happen to them ... and to the New Japan?

In America a storm of protest deluged the White House. Overnight the country was torn with dispute. There were demands that President Truman be impeached. In California he was hanged in effigy.

Draft officials resigned on protest. Flags were flown at half-mast. Workmen staged protest walkouts. Some of them picketed the White House. Churches held special services to pray for guidance for the country.

During the six years of their unusual relationship MacArthur and the Emperor had become cordial friends. Now, unprecedentedly, the Emperor came to bid him good-by. Tears filled his eyes as he took MacArthur's hand in both of his. He spoke no English, MacArthur no Japanese; but no words were needed to express the depths of the Emperor's gratitude for MacArthur's benevolent stewardship, and of his sense of personal loss.

Friendly messages from all over the world poured into MacArthur's headquarters. An invitation to address a meeting of the two Houses of Congress reached him. The date set was April 19. Although it meant leaving Japan only five days after being relieved, MacArthur was ready.

As early as the afternoon before he was scheduled to leave, thousands of Japanese began to gather along the eight-mile route from the Embassy to Haneda Airport. They waited through the cold night for a final glimpse of the man whose wise guidance had transformed their lives, and to show him their respect and affection. As the morning of April 17 dawned, thousands more joined them. Some had walked or pedaled bicycles all night.

At 6:28 A.M. the MacArthurs left the Embassy. It was the beginning of eight miles of massed humanity—children waving American and Japanese flags, shouts of "sayonara," men and women in tears. Then "Macassa" was gone.

At the airport a battery of howitzers fired a nineteen-gun salute. MacArthur inspected the waiting Honor Guard and saluted the colors. Then, with his wife and son, he walked down the long line of friends and dignitaries, shaking hands and saying good-by.

As they reached the door of the plane, and turned to wave to the crowd, a band began playing "Auld Lang Syne." Then the doors closed and the crowd fell back. In a few minutes the *Bataan* was airborne. The journey homeward had begun.

MacArthur had no inkling of the welcome which was awaiting him in America. His time had been so completely taken up with preparations for his departure that he had only a general idea of the thousands of cables and telephone calls which had flooded the circuits, all expressing sympathy and understanding.

Between the press of personal details and last-minute duties, he had worked on the address which he was to present to the assembled Congress. In America he expected to have at least one full day of privacy during which he could revise and complete it.

"Court," he had said to General Whitney, "please arrange the trip so that we will arrive in San Francisco and New York after dark, to enable us to slip into a hotel without being noticed."

As the *Bataan* spanned the first leg of their journey, from Tokyo to Honolulu, MacArthur worked on his address. It was shaping up as he wanted it—not as a denunciation of the

President and his advisers, but as a sober statement of the hopelessness of America's position in Asia under the Administration's policies.

In Honolulu, MacArthur received the first indication of the warm welcome which he could expect at home. But the welcome in Honolulu in no way prepared him for what lay ahead.

It was dark when the *Bataan* swung over the Golden Gate bridge, and the glittering panoply of lights spread out beyond it, for its approach to the San Francisco airport. It was Arthur's first glimpse of his native land, and his eyes widened in wonder as he took in the scene below him. MacArthur put his arm around his son's shoulders.

"Well, Arthur, my boy," he said, "we are home at last."

The ramp had hardly been placed and the door opened when the crowd surged forward. It broke past police lines and swarmed up to the plane, everyone eager to get a close look at the tall, amazed figure in the familiar cap, and at his wife and son.

Governor Warren and Mayor Robinson greeted the MacArthurs with a sincere warmth that reflected the feelings of the whole mass of humanity that surrounded the plane. With difficulty the police made way for them to waiting cars.

MacArthur was overwhelmed. Cheering people lined the route into San Francisco, and more cheering thousands packed the area around his hotel. It was but the beginning of weeks of similar ovations in cities all across the land. It was a hero's welcome. All of the sense of sadness which had pervaded him disappeared completely in the face of this welcome . . . this spontaneous manifestation of the public's belief that he had been wronged.

At the hotel friends waited to see MacArthur. Among them were men high in the inner councils of the Republican party. In his suite they sounded him out as to his availability as a Presidential candidate. He had no such desire.

Next morning he received an official greeting at the City Hall. He used the opportunity to set the record straight.

"I have been asked if I intended to enter politics," he said, in his short speech of appreciation. "My reply was no. I have no political aspirations whatsoever. I do not intend to run for political office, and I hope that my name will never be used in a political way. The only politics I have is contained in a single phrase known well to all of you—God Bless America."

It was after midnight, Washington time, when the *Bataan* landed at the nation's capital. Despite the hour, again huge crowds waited to greet him. Again it was with difficulty that the police finally cut a path for the party to leave the airport.

The next afternoon cheering thousands lined Pennsylvania Avenue as MacArthur was driven to the Capitol. Promptly at noon a committee from both Houses of Congress escorted him into the Chamber of the House of Representatives. Deafening applause greeted him.

As he stood on the rostrum, with some of the nation's greatest orators waiting to hear him, he realized that, all over the world, millions would hear and weigh his words. It was a mighty challenge.

Calmly he paid respectful homage to the great body which had invited him to appear before it. He made it clear that he was not seizing upon this opportunity to castigate anyone . . . that he had no partisan purpose in view.

"I trust, therefore, that you will do me the justice of receiving that which I have to say as solely expressing the considered viewpoint of a fellow American. I address you with neither rancor nor bitterness in the fading twilight of life with but one purpose in mind—to serve my country."

A hush had fallen over the chamber; but now, as MacArthur paused, a thunderclap of applause broke out from both sides of the aisle. When he resumed, he began to develop the issues involved and to emphasize their world significance.

"The issues are global," he warned them, "and so interlocked that to consider the problems of one sector oblivious to those of another is but to court disaster for the whole."

He explained the strategic relationship of the Pacific area to the security of the United States . . . and of Formosa's importance in the defensive scheme . . . of the tragic loss of China. He lauded the people of the Philippines, and the progress which the Japanese had made in earning a place among the democratic nations. Carefully he outlined his rejected plans for winning the war in Korea. Weighed carefully, his words made it appear extremely doubtful that anyone high in our government had ever actually believed that victory in Korea —no matter by what means—would set off World War III. There had obviously been other motives involved in the Administration's refusal to allow him to defeat the enemy.

Steadily his resonant tones filled the hushed chamber. He paused only when he was forced to wait out the frequent bursts of spontaneous applause. In their very sincerity his words made all of the issues extremely clear, more effectively than deliberate castigation could have done.

War, he warned them, must be abolished if civilization is to survive. The advances of science had made it too terrible. But while war is here, he insisted, it must be fought to win.

He warned of the dangers of further appeasement of Russia and Red China.

"War's very object is victory," he reminded them, "not indecision." And he added the words which Minority Leader Martin had read in this same chamber: "In war, there is no substitute for victory!"

His closing words have become a national byword.

"I am closing my fifty-two years of military service," he said. "When I joined the Army, even before the turn of the century, it was the fulfillment of all my boyish hopes and dreams. The world has turned over many times since I took the oath on the Plain at West Point, and hopes and dreams have all since vanished, but I still remember the refrain of one of the most popular barrack ballads of that day, which proclaimed most proudly that old soldiers never die; they just fade away. And like the old soldier of that ballad, I now close my military career and just fade away, an old soldier who tried to do his duty as God gave him the light to see that duty. Good-by."

In the momentary hush which preceded thunderous applause, no open mind could doubt that, in the clarity of his vision, he had seen disaster strike—from within. In Douglas MacArthur there dwelt the high ideals of loyalty and patriotism of earlier decades. None could doubt that, no matter what the personal sacrifice, his country came first.

18.

"I BID YOU FAREWELL"

Ӿ   Never in all its turbulent history of hearty welcomes had New York greeted a returning hero with such mad acclaim. The route from the airport to the Waldorf-Astoria, which was to become the MacArthurs' permanent home, was crowded with cheering people. Men, women, and children, young and old, rich and poor, jammed the sidewalks and crowded the thousands of windows. As the cavalcade entered each block, the cry was taken up all over again: "There he is! There he is!"

At the hotel masses of mail awaited him. More than 150,-000 letters and twenty thousand telegrams had already arrived, and more poured in by the sackload.

Settled in their suite, the MacArthurs hoped to live quiet,

normal lives. But it was not yet the General's privilege to simply "fade away." Another duty called.

The public's angry protests stirred Congress to inquire into the real reason for his recall. He was asked to appear before a joint session of the Senate Committees on Armed Services and Foreign Affairs.

His testimony was a revelation to the members of the committees. No longer bound by his official relationships with the President, the hearing enabled him to speak freely upon matters which had long been of grave concern to him.

Although the purpose of the hearing had been solely to inquire into the military situation in the Far East, and the circumstances surrounding MacArthur's recall, it soon became apparent that there were matters of greater significance to explore.

MacArthur had been prevented from delivering the *coup de grâce* to the Red Chinese armies massed against his own forces . . . and, perhaps, to Mao's brutal hold on the Chinese people. But now he was able to open the eyes of the American people to the frightening extent of the Communist threat in Asia, and to the failure of the Administration's policies in Korea.

For three days, unaided by documents or notes, MacArthur answered questions which covered a vast scope of Asian history, of American foreign policy, and of relative military power lucidly and without hesitation. Calmly he answered all questions and managed to retain a nonpartisan position.

When his testimony was completed, Senator Richard B. Russell of Georgia, who conducted the hearing, expressed both the appreciation of the Joint Committees and their collective wonder at his amazing grasp of affairs.

As other witnesses followed him, their testimony, too, revealed the shocking ineptitude of the Administration's Asian policies, and the extent to which Red China had been aided by the deliberate betrayal of Chiang Kai-shek, Communism's oldest foe in Asia. They vindicated completely MacArthur's judgment in significant matters—Yalta, Formosa, Nationalist China, Korea, the inroads of Communism in Asia.

Two memorable visits highlighted the MacArthurs' first few days at home.

On April 27 they drove from Chicago to Milwaukee, past knots of cheering people, to visit his family home. Again a tremendous ovation greeted them.

On the 30th they visited Murfreesboro, Tennessee. But this was "Miss Jean's" day. Proudly thousands of people from all over Tennessee joined her family in welcoming Jean Faircloth MacArthur back to her old home town. It was a loving tribute to a home-town girl they all adored.

In a short talk at the stadium of the Middle Tennessee State College, MacArthur took his cue.

"I am no stranger to the South," he told the Tennesseans. "Born in Arkansas of a Virginia mother, I grew up with the sound of *Dixie* and a rebel yell ringing in my ears. Pop was on the other side, but had the good sense to surrender to my mother."

There was great hilarity when an old beau made a distinctive presentation—a six-star gold medal, which elevated Jean MacArthur to a rank higher than her husband's.

Back in New York, MacArthur received countless invitations to visit cities and towns, to receive honors of various kinds. Politely he declined them. He believed that he could, at last, simply "fade away."

With the first leisure that he had enjoyed in many years, he began to study the new, and somehow different America to which he had returned. What he learned was not encouraging. Complacency appeared to have dulled the people's comprehension of the dangers which menaced the land. He determined to embark upon a one-man crusade in an attempt to awaken the American people to these dangers.

His first speech was in Chicago, in Soldier Field. His approach was rigidly nonpartisan: ". . . the enemy bullets have no respect for political affiliation," he told the wildly cheering crowd, "and strike down the son of a Democrat as surely as the son of a Republican."

Some segments of the press criticized his crusade. It was wrong, some editors stated, for a military man to involve himself in purely governmental affairs. He took no notice. He had never accepted the politically inspired contention that a man who dons his country's uniform must give up his rights as a citizen . . . that he must abandon any active interest in his country's welfare.

MacArthur rejected firmly all suggestions that he become a Presidential candidate. But when he was asked to be the keynote speaker at the Republican convention, he accepted.

When he entered the convention hall, MacArthur received a thunderous ovation. His speech brought another sustained round of cheering and applause. A wild demonstration followed, but he slipped out and returned home. He had no desire to capitalize upon the enthusiasm which his appearance had created.

In the fall of 1949 Mr. James M. Rand had inquired into the possibility of acquiring MacArthur's services when he had completed his active career. Although impressed with

Remington Rand enterprises, MacArthur was too deeply concerned with the details of reorganizing the Japanese government to consider leaving active service.

When he had completed his crusade, and delivered his address to the Republican National Convention, the desire to simply fade away into complete inactivity deserted him. His whole life had been a series of challenges. He welcomed a new one. So, on August 1, 1952, he assumed the demanding chairmanship of the Board of Remington Rand.

His uniform was packed away now, along with his famous cap.

"I guess I shan't be wearing it again, Court, until they carry me to Arlington Cemetery," he had said to General Whitney.

His acute mind and tireless energies were now directed into new fields. He was keenly aware of the vast changes which were stirring the industrial world to new endeavors. He could envision the goals to which scientific achievements were pointing the way.

As he became more closely acquainted with the scope of scientific progress, he developed an entirely new concept of war. The oldest soldier of his time was readily adaptable to change. But he was not reconciled to appeasement.

To the Association of Graduates of West Point, at the Founders' Day dinner in 1953, he addressed a warning.

". . . oblivious to the lessons of military history and the American traditions, a new concept has arisen which tends to disavow victory as the combat objective. . . . The result can be nothing but failure, nothing to repay the terrible human sacrifice of war. If this nation is to survive . . . we must reject the counsels of fear which strange and alien doctrines are attempting to force upon us. We must proclaim again and again an invincible adherence to the proposition that, in war, there can be no substitute for victory."

He chose the occasion of the dedication of the MacArthur Memorial Park and monument, in Los Angeles, to deliver a strong plea for peace. Even the New York *Herald Tribune,* one of his most consistent critics, hailed his declaration that "war has become an anachronism" as one which made "the simplest and most familiar things stand out as if they had been seen for the first time." The old soldier, it added, "never ... seemed a grander figure."

It was MacArthur's seventy-fifth birthday. From all over the world messages of congratulation poured in from heads of state, from leaders in every field of human endeavor, and from obscure people everywhere.

Earlier the Illinois Department of the Veterans of Foreign Wars had urged that, on his birthday, the rank of "General of the Armies" be bestowed upon MacArthur. Only General Pershing had ever received that honor. It was a just and fitting tribute, the veterans believed, because he had been "relieved of his command for placing his country above all else." The nomination was not made.

In February, 1957, Field Marshal Viscount Alanbrooke, wartime Chief of the British Imperial General Staff, created a furor of feeling, both at home and in America, when, in his published war diaries, he rated MacArthur as the "greatest general of World War II." He saw in him "the summation of all military skills," who "certainly showed a far greater strategic grasp than Marshall." Eisenhower's success he attributed to "personal charm" and to "a greater share of luck than most of us receive in life."

It came at a time when the tide of professional opinion had begun to turn. Even some of MacArthur's severest critics had come to admit that he had been right ... that the war in Korea had been the right war in the right place to smash Communism in Asia at relatively small cost, and to destroy both Red China and the carefully planned Soviet timetable of conquest. They had begun to recognize the truth of his contention that Europe's war was being fought in Asia.

The MacArthurs lived simply and quietly. Although Arthur had not chosen to perpetuate the traditions which had brought both his father and his grandfather fame, he and his father were no less close in their idealisms. Should war come, his father knew that Arthur would be among the first to go. What kind of leadership would he have, the General wondered. Perhaps he had this in mind when he went up to West Point, on May 12, 1962, to receive the Sylvanus Thayer Award for services to the nation.

It was, he had decided, to be his last visit—his farewell to his old Corps. As he watched the gray-clad companies assemble on the Plain, he thought of that day, more than sixty years before, when he had become one of "the Long Gray Line." He had never swerved from the oath which he had taken that day—an oath to protect his country from her enemies. Through the years he had fought them all.

As the last company reached its place in line, and silence fell across the Plain, the reviewing party came forward— General MacArthur, General Westmoreland, Superintendent of the Academy, and Cadet James Rayford Ellis, First Captain of the Corps. Behind them a soldier bore the five-star flag of a General of the Army.

The drums and trumpets sounded the ruffles and flourishes;

then the band sounded *The General.* The three took their places in a silvered jeep, Cadet Ellis standing beside the driver, the Generals behind the handrail in the rear.

Slowly the jeep moved to the right of the brigade. There it turned; and, as the band played softly and the Corps of Cadets stood rocklike in the warm spring sun, it moved slowly down the long, gray line in front of the dipping guidons.

Closely packed around the field, thirty-seven thousand spectators watched as the party completed the "ride around" and returned to their places for the age-old ceremony.

The command "Pass in review!" echoed across the Plain, and the colorful "march past" began. Standing at attention, MacArthur watched—perhaps a bit wistfully—the leading companies march by. When the colors passed, he whipped off his hat and held it over his left breast in his last salute to the colors of his beloved Corps.

When the last company had passed, he shook hands with First Captain Ellis, and complimented him on the appearance of the Brigade. Then he turned away to greet old friends.

Lunch was a colorful affair. In the great cadet mess hall, its walls hung with the colors of gallant regiments and with portraits of superintendents long since dead, the whole Corps—twenty-three hundred strong—was seated. At a ceremonial head table, set under a balcony on which Mrs. MacArthur and the other ladies were seated, MacArthur chatted pleasantly with General Westmoreland and Lieutenant General Leslie R. Groves, who was to make the presentation. If MacArthur gave any thought to the address which he was about to make, it was not apparent. His manner was relaxed, cordial, almost gay.

When lunch ended, General Groves delivered a brief résumé of MacArthur's many distinguished services to his country and made the presentation. Graciously MacArthur thanked him.

As Groves sat down, and MacArthur turned to face his audience, an expectant hush fell over the hall. No one knew what he intended to say. He had no notes, no prepared script.

For a moment, his eyes roved over the sea of young faces before him. Those nearest to him could see his eyes twinkle, and a faint smile touch his lips.

"As I was leaving the hotel this morning," he began, "a doorman asked me, 'Where are you bound for, General?' and when I replied, 'West Point,' he remarked, 'Beautiful place. Have you ever been there before?'"

A gale of laughter swept through the hall, then the hush fell again. When MacArthur resumed, all traces of humor were gone.

"No human being could fail to be deeply moved by such a tribute as this," he told them. "Coming from a profession I have served so long, and a people I have loved so well, it fills me with an emotion I cannot express. But this award is not intended primarily to honor a personality, but to symbolize a great moral code—the code of conduct and chivalry of those who guard this beloved land of culture and ancient descent. That is the meaning of this medallion. For all eyes and for all time, it is an expression of the ethics of the American soldier. That I should be integrated in this way with so noble an ideal arouses a sense of pride and yet of humility which will be with me always."

He spoke slowly, and with all of the eloquence of his younger days. Although he was eighty-two, he appeared younger. He stood easily erect, and his voice had much of its old dramatic impact.

"Duty—Honor—Country. Three hallowed words reverently dictate what you ought to be, what you can be, what you will be. They are your rallying points: to build courage when courage seems to fail; to regain faith when there seems to be little cause for faith; to create hope when hope becomes forlorn. Unhappily I possess neither that eloquence of diction, that poetry of imagination, that brilliance of metaphor to tell you all that they mean. The unbelievers will say that they are but words, but a slogan, but a flamboyant phrase. Every pedant, every demagogue, every cynic, every hypocrite, every troublemaker, and, I am sorry to say, some others of an entirely different character will try to down-grade them even to the extent of mockery and ridicule.

"But these are some things which they do. They build your basic character, they mold you for your future roles as the custodians of the nation's defense, they make you strong enough to know when you are weak, and brave enough to face yourself when you are afraid. They teach you to be proud and unbending in honest failure, but humble and gentle in success; not to substitute words for actions, nor to seek the path of comfort, but to face the stress and spur of difficulty and challenge; to learn to stand up in the storm, but to have compassion on those who fall; to master yourself before you seek to master others; to have a heart that is clean, a goal that is high; to learn to laugh yet never forget how to weep; to reach into the future yet never neglect the past; to be serious yet never to take yourself too seriously; to be modest so that you will remember the simplicity of true greatness, the open mind of true wisdom, the meekness of true strength. They give you a temper of the will, a quality of the imagination, a vigor of the emotions, a freshness of the deep springs of life, a temperamental predominance of courage over timidity, an appetite for adventure over love of ease. They create in your heart the sense of wonder, the unfailing hope of what next, and the joy and inspiration of life. They teach you in this way to be an officer and a gentleman."

He paused for a moment, and in the unbroken silence not a cadet in the whole vast hall failed to realize that the words were directed straight at him.

"And what sort of soldiers are those you are to lead? Are they reliable, are they brave, are they capable of victory? Their story is known to all of you; it is the story of the American man-at-arms. My estimate of him was formed on the battlefield many, many years ago, and has never changed. I regarded him then as I regard him now—as one of the world's noblest figures, not only as one of the finest military characters but also as one of the most stainless. . . . He needs no eulogy from me or from any man. . . . In twenty campaigns, on a hundred battlefields, around a thousand campfires, I have witnessed that enduring fortitude, that patriotic self-abnegation, and that invincible determination which had carved his statue in the hearts of his people.

"In memory's eye, I can see those staggering columns of the First World War . . . on many a weary march from dripping dusk to drizzling dawn . . . slogging ankle-deep through the mire to form grimly for the attack, blue-lipped, covered with sludge and mud, chilled by the wind and rain; driving home to their objective, and, for many, to the judgment seat of God. I do not know the dignity of their birth but I do know the glory of their death. They died unquestioning, uncomplaining, with faith in their hearts, and on their lips the hope that we would go on to victory. Always for them—Duty —Honor—Country; always their blood and sweat and tears as we sought the way and the light and the truth."

Again he paused, as though in reverence to the gallant dead. Not a sound was audible; not a listener stirred.

"And after twenty years, on the other side of the globe," the sonorous voice went on, "again the filth of murky foxholes, the stench of ghostly trenches, the slime of dripping dugouts . . . the loneliness and utter desolation of jungle trails, the bitterness of long separation from those they loved and cherished, the deadly pestilence of tropical disease, the horror of stricken areas of war; their resolute and determined defense, their swift and sure attack, their indomitable purpose, their complete and decisive victory—always victory. Always through the bloody haze of their last reverberating shot, the vision of gaunt, ghastly men reverently following your password of Duty—Honor—Country.

"The code which those words perpetuate embraces the highest moral laws. . . . The soldier, above all other men, is required to practice the greatest act of religious training— sacrifice. In battle and in the face of danger and death, he discloses those divine attributes which his Maker gave him when he created man in His own image."

He explained that they faced a new world—"the beginning of another epoch in the long story of mankind"—the space age; that they would see a staggering evolution, and that undreamed-of advances would be made in the sciences and in the explorations of outer space; that they would learn strange words and see unfathomed mysteries revealed.

But always, he reminded them, "your mission remains fixed, determined, inviolable—it is to win wars. Everything in your professional career is but corollary to this vital dedication. All other public purposes, all other public projects, all other public needs, great or small, will find others for their accomplishment; but you are the ones who are trained to fight; yours is the profession of arms—the will to win, the sure knowledge that in war there is no substitute for victory."

Let others debate the controversial issues, he counseled them, and let others decide the merits of governmental issues. "Your guidepost stands out like a tenfold beacon in the night!

"You are the leaven which binds together the entire fabric of our national system of defense," he reminded them. "From your ranks come the great captains who hold the nation's destiny in their hands the moment the war tocsin sounds. The Long Gray Line has never failed us. Were you to do so, a million ghosts in olive drab, in brown khaki, in blue and gray, would rise from their white crosses thundering those magic words—Duty—Honor—Country.

"This does not mean that you are warmongers. On the contrary, the soldier above all other people prays for peace, for he must suffer and bear the deepest wounds and scars of war. But always in our ears ring the ominous words of Plato that 'only the dead have seen the end of war.' "

There was a longer pause, and his eyes seemed to linger on the hanging colors—the colors of regiments which he had known in far places through the strife-torn years. When he resumed, a touch of sadness seemed to cloud his features.

"The shadows are lengthening for me now," he told them. "The twilight is here. My days of old have vanished tone and tint; they have gone glimmering through the dreams of things that were. Their memory is one of wondrous beauty, watered by tears, and coaxed and caressed by the smiles of yesterday. I listen vainly for the witching melody of faint bugles blowing reveille, of far drums beating the long roll. In my dreams I hear again the crash of guns, the rattle of musketry, the strange, mournful mutter of the battlefield. But in the evening of my memory, always I come back to West Point. Always there echoes and re-echoes Duty—Honor —Country.

"Today marks my final roll call with you, but I want you to know that when I cross the river my last conscious thoughts will be of the Corps, and the Corps, and the Corps."

A little sigh escaped him as his discerning eyes roved again over the sea of eager young faces before him. He no longer wondered what kind of leadership his son might have. He knew. The tenets of Duty and Honor and Country were written clearly upon each face. These clean, embryo soldiers of the Republic would accept no false doctrines. They would lower neither his country's standards nor its flag. They were The Long Gray Line. He was content.

There was pride in his heart when he said to them simply: "I bid you farewell!"

BIBLIOGRAPHY

BOOKS

DeWeerd, Harvey A., *Great Soldiers of World War II*, W. W. Norton and Company, New York, 1944

Eichelberger, Robert L., and Mackaye, Milton, *Our Jungle Road to Tokyo*, The Viking Press, Inc., New York, 1950

Ganoe, William A., *MacArthur Close-Up*, Vantage Press, New York, 1962

Gunther, John, *The Riddle of MacArthur*, Harper and Brothers, New York, 1951

Halsey, William F., *Admiral Halsey's Story*, McGraw-Hill Book Company, Inc., New York, 1947

Hersey, John, *Men on Bataan*, Alfred A. Knopf, Inc., New York, 1942

Hunt, Frazier, *MacArthur and the War Against Japan*, Charles Scribner's Sons, New York, 1944.

—— *The Untold Story of Douglas MacArthur*, The Devin-Adair Co., New York, 1954

Kelley, Frank, and Ryan, Cornelius, *MacArthur: Man of Action*, Doubleday and Co., Inc., New York, 1950

Kenney, George C., *General Kenney Reports*, Duell, Sloan and Pearce, Inc., New York, 1949

—— *The MacArthur I Knew*, Duell, Sloan and Pearce, Inc., New York, 1951

Kodama, Yoshio, *I Was Defeated*, Robert Booth and Taro Fukuda, Tokyo, 1951

173

Krueger, Walter, *From Down Under to Nippon,* Combat Forces Press, Washington, 1953

Leahy, William D., *I Was There,* Whittlesey House, New York, 1950

Lee, Clark, and Henschel, Richard, *Douglas MacArthur,* Henry Holt and Co., New York, 1952

Pershing, John J., *My Experiences in the World War,* Frederick A. Stokes Co., New York, 1931

Reilly, Henry J., *Americans All, the Rainbow at War,* The F. J. Heer Printing Co., Columbus, Ohio, 1936

Romulo, Carlos P., *I Saw the Fall of the Philippines,* Doubleday, Doran and Company, Inc., New York, 1942

Toland, John, *But Not in Shame,* Random House, Inc., New York, 1961

Wainwright, Jonathan M., *General Wainwright's Story,* ed. by Robert Consadine, Doubleday and Company, Inc., New York, 1946

Waldrop, Frank C., *MacArthur on War,* Duell, Sloan and Pearce, Inc., New York, 1942

Whitney, Courtney, *MacArthur and His Rendezvous With History,* Alfred A. Knopf, Inc., New York, 1956

Willoughby, Charles A., and Chamberlain, John, *MacArthur: 1941– 1951,* McGraw-Hill Book Company, Inc., New York, 1954

NEWSPAPERS

Army Times
Atlanta Journal
Chattanooga Times
Chicago Tribune
Mainichi

New York Herald Tribune
Nippon Times
St. Louis Post-Dispatch
Stars and Stripes
Washington Star

MAGAZINES

American Legion Magazine
Army and Navy Journal
Army and Navy Register
Collier's
Current Biography
Current History
Fanfare (Japan)

Life
Look
New Yorker
Saturday Evening Post
Time
U.S. News and World Report

DOCUMENTS

Historical Register and Dictionary of the U.S. Army, Francis B. Heitman, Government Printing Office, Washington, 1903

Senate Document No. 69, 82d Congress, 1st Session, Government Printing Office, Washington, 1951

War of the Rebellion, Records of the Union and Confederate Armies, Government Printing Office, Washington, 1880–1901